TUDOR
GLOUCESTERSHIRE

Fairford Church: largely rebuilt in the early 16th century by John and Edmund Tame.

TUDOR
GLOUCESTERSHIRE

Joan Johnson

ALAN SUTTON &
GLOUCESTERSHIRE COUNTY LIBRARY
1985

The County Library Series is published jointly by Alan Sutton Publishing Limited and Gloucestershire County Library. All correspondence relating to the series should be addressed to:

Alan Sutton Publishing Limited
30 Brunswick Road
Gloucester GL1 1JJ

First published 1985

British Library Cataloguing in Publication Data

Johnson, Joan, 1915–
    Tudor Gloucestershire.
    1. Gloucestershire—History
    I. Title
    942.4'105   DA670.G5

ISBN 0-86299-222-2

Printed in Great Britain.

Contents

List of Illustrations

Except where otherwise stated, plates have been reproduced from pictures in private collections.

Introduction

The history of Gloucestershire during the Tudor period is not unlike one of the rich tapestries that adorned the walls of so many of its homes at the time. The foreground is peopled with colourful personalities, prominent in national as well as local affairs – soldiers and seamen like the Berkeleys, Brydges and Wynters: diplomats and successful businessmen such as the Chamberlaynes, Hicks, Duttons and Leighs: eminent churchmen like William Tyndale, Hugh Latimer and John Hooper. The stories of all these are woven into the events of the reigns of the Tudor sovereigns, three of whom – Henry VII, Henry VIII and Elizabeth I – themselves added colour and excitement to the lives of Gloucestershire people during the course of royal progresses here. The background of the tapestry is crammed with evidence of the fullness of life in the area – prosperous trade and agriculture, well planned houses and gardens, and the pleasures of hunting, hawking, fairs, drama and dancing.

Narrowly interpreted, the Tudor period comprises the years between the accession of Henry VII in 1485 and the death of Elizabeth I, his grand-daughter, in 1603. But historical periods cannot be as sharply defined as this, since generations of people overlap and one set of circumstances emerges gradually from another, so that progress is continuous and often imperceptible except in retrospect. Events such as a royal birth, a battle or the signing of a peace treaty can be pinpointed as to date; but by contrast, social and economic developments have to be measured over long periods and may even seem to lack a definite beginning and end. Moreover, in general, historical events occur in logical sequence and have logical consequences, so that the consideration of a particular happening inevitably prompts a query as to what led up to it and what resulted from it.

Looking back from the standpoint of 1485, it is clear that the country was nearing, and had in some respects already reached, the end of an era. Constitutionally and politically, the struggle between the mediaeval kings and their over-mighty subjects had culminated in the Wars of the Roses – a lesson to both sides – with two major battles, Tewkesbury in 1468 and Bosworth in 1485, deciding both the immediate issue of who was to rule the country and the long term outcome of how he was to do this. Even before these wars broke out however, and certainly by the end of them, the

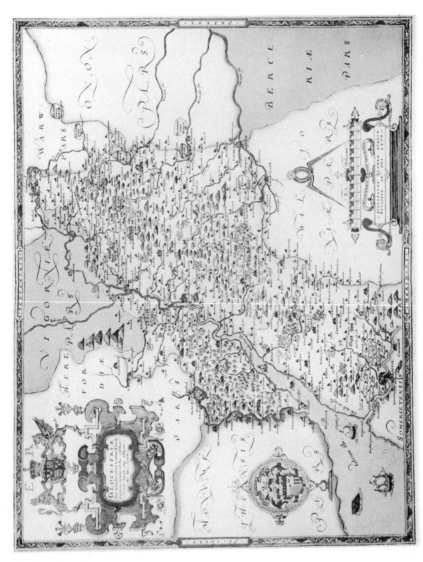

Saxton's Map of Gloucestershire (1579): the earliest delineation of the county.

weaknesses in the structure of feudalism (which had determined all aspects of national life in the Middle Ages) were visible, and its ultimate disappearance from England inevitable. And just as a new style of architecture was beginning to introduce more light and greater elaboration into ecclesiastical and domestic buildings, so men seemed to be redirecting their outlook and hopes away from the circumscribed prospects of earlier times to the potentially wider ones of the future.

And the view ahead in 1485 was definitely promising, with the country under a young king, filled with an energy and ambition that was to infect his subjects in due course, and fire them with the courage and confidence to face and exploit new situations successfully. Already also, although it was not yet realised, the atmosphere over Europe, charged with the force of new discoveries in the spheres of art and learning, was beginning to drift into England, and to provide a nation emerging from infancy, with pleasures and excitements such as impressionable, energetic adolescents could delight in without tiring. The future seemed promising too for the impatient ambitious men who had begun to find the dual authorities of feudalism and the mediaeval church irksome, and were seeking ways of circumventing inconvenient and, (to them) excessive demands on their time, efforts and resources.

While having its own distinctive characteristics, the 16th century was in some ways a transitional period, bridging the gap between remote mediaevalism and the more modern 17th century. By comparison with what had gone before, the mood of the 16th century was one of vigour and enterprise, with some sections of society at least, ready to contemplate and accept unprecedented changes: the leading roles in national affairs taken over from armoured barons and their liveried retainers, by peace-seeking sovereigns advised by astute ministers: and the nation's fortunes determined not on the field of battle but in the Council Chamber. During the course of the century, in the congenial atmosphere of peace and prosperity, many able and gifted men made their contribution to the country's progress and prestige: England acquired a new form of religion and the beginning of an overseas empire: and finally under Elizabeth, having defeated the Spanish Armada, emerged as a leader among the other states of Europe.

But a break with the past such as these changes implied could not be achieved without strain. Progressive action tends to produce a reaction, and in any case the forces of conservatism in England were strong, and even while reconciling themselves to change, many people looked back over their shoulders wistfully and went on regretting the past. Growth also can be painful, and somewhat discouraging to all but the toughest, especially when new situations produce new problems for which there is no known remedy. To those in the lead the challenges of the 16th century were exciting and irresistible, the prizes glittering and well worth the risks

John Falkner, cap-maker, who rose to be Mayor of Gloucester.

involved. To the more cautious and fearful, who were drawn along in their wake, the dangers seemed to outweigh possible gains; but there was no standing still in that highly competitive society, so those who did not advance necessarily fell behind, and suffered in even greater numbers than those who were toppled from the pinnacles of success by overweening confidence and ambition.

As well as change and progress, the country also saw the beginning of a shift in political and social emphases during the 16th century. Having willingly acquiesced in the authority of an efficient government and exalted the Tudor monarchs to the position of benevolent guardians of England's welfare, the people began to relax, experiment and enjoy the fruits of their enterprise, to such an extent that the rigid social order, which had hitherto been regarded as essential to the continuance of their world, no longer seemed sacrosanct. Greater physical mobility, which accompanied times of peace and opportunity, was parallelled by social mobility, reflected in the rise of hard-working craftsmen, traders and lawyers to gentry status, and the decline of some members of the upper classes who were failing to maintain the fortunes necessary to their standard of living. To be a success in the eyes of the world and according to contemporary values was becoming more important than to observe the moral obligations imposed by an active, old fashioned conscience.

The achievement of personal ambitions bred confidence, so that by the end of the century some bold men were beginning to question the need for an all-powerful, omniscient sovereign, and to argue that ultimate political power should lie with those of proven worth and ability, and not necessarily where tradition and precedent dictated. The extent to which the country in general and many men in particular were indebted to the Tudor monarchs for favours and encouragement, ceased to be acknowledged; and instead, the dual influences of the Renaissance and Reformation (which had done so much to give men the courage of their convictions) began to prompt individuals into bold speech and daring behaviour such as their grandparents neither could nor would have contemplated. The attitude of the House of Commons under Elizabeth I illustrated this tendency very clearly, and was a forewarning of what was to happen in the next century.

The rate and extent of change in the 16th century varied enormously according to which part of the country was under consideration. In general, areas furthest from London were slowest to respond to the times, but Gloucestershire was not one of these. Geographically within easy reach of the Thames valley, and commercially in regular contact with London, Bristol and the Midlands, the county had been comparatively advanced both economically and socially during the Middle Ages. In consequence the new ideas of the 16th century, in respect of religion for instance, did not seem as revolutionary in Gloucestershire as elsewhere: and already here, since the 14th century, some social mobility had been visible, with men moving upwards from the status of freeholder or craftsman to that of the gentry. The county had in fact acquired some of the resilience that enabled it to take the shocks of the 16th century in its stride and saved it from any major disturbances such as broke out in the south-west peninsula and East Anglia. Necessarily, the dissolution of the monasteries was a major event because so much of the land in Gloucestershire had belonged to the monks: but there were many buyers eager to take on the monastic estates, and in due course others ready to assume the educational and charitable responsibilities of the monks. Among the purchasers of the land were newcomers to the scene, who at this point began to put down roots in the

Gloucester: increasing in significance during the 16th century.

county, were absorbed into its economic and social structure, and thereafter benefited its life with their goodwill, experience and expertise.

Whether they belonged to old established families or were newcomers to the area, men of all ranks were aware of the changes and challenges of the times they were living in, and to the extent of their capacities took advantage of the opportunities that came their way. Thus, Gloucestershire towns grew in size, wealth and economic significance, and provided a standard of life highly desirable to many who were trying to better themselves. In the countryside, methods of farming were being improved and the returns from land increased to meet the needs of owners who all wanted a greater degree of comfort and sophistication in their lives. In the course of the century the county lost many beautiful monastic buildings and useful religious foundations, but there were compensations for these in the additions made to parish churches, and investments put into new schools, almshouses and other charitable institutions. These were dark times also for some people, victims of religious intolerance, inflation, trade fluctuations and bad harvests, but on the whole Gloucestershire advanced under Tudor rule, a fact that was to explain its significance during the crisis of the Civil War in the next century.

1
The State of England in General . . .

As a result of the defeat and death of Richard III at the Battle of Bosworth, Henry Tudor was enabled to take possession of the crown of England in 1485, but he would not have dared to claim that his victory constituted a legal title. Even on a hereditary basis he was not much better qualified, because although his family line could be traced back to John of Gaunt and his third wife Katherine Swynford, the marriage of these forebears had occurred too late to legitimise the issue of it – and legitimacy was an important consideration in mediaeval minds. So, from the outset, Henry was in a position where he had to justify himself to survive. Happily, both for himself and the country, he was able to do this.

As well as the statesmanlike and military qualities of his Lancastrian forebear, Henry inherited Welsh shrewdness from his father's family, the Tudors, and aesthetic intellectualism from his mother's family, the Beauforts. Through personal experience he had learned the importance of a powerful following, and at the same time the dangers inherent in this; how, when faced with promising opportunities, even basically loyal and well-meaning men might be tempted to waver in their allegiance; and how, in troubled, dangerous times, decisiveness and a single-minded pursuit of one's aims could be more impressive and achieve more in the estimation of others, than leniency or reasonable moderation.

Having survived the Wars of the Roses and subsequent exile during the reigns of Edward IV and Richard III, Henry returned to England in 1485 conscious of the dangers that could attend the exercise of kingly rule here, and at the same time determined to rise above these. From the start he showed that he had the ability, common to all the Tudors, except perhaps his granddaughter Mary, to gauge the climate of opinion among his subjects and to interpret correctly their needs and wishes at any particular moment. This foreknowledge of public feeling was to make it possible for Henry VII and his successors to produce seemingly as their own, ideas that were certain to be popular. At the same time there was room for expediency and opportunism in Tudor policy, a willingness to modify plans if circumstances demanded, a readiness to take a promising chance if it offered. All-important was the need to ensure continuing popular support.

The country to which Henry succeeded was less densely populated than it

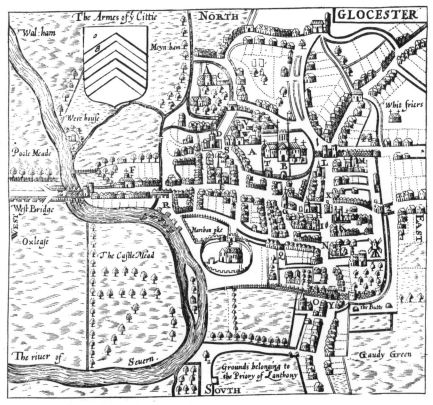

The chequer-board pattern of Gloucester, shown in a map of 1610.

had been a century before, owing to the virulence of the Black Death, and by contrast with other European countries it seemed to have abounding potential, with extensive undeveloped and underdeveloped areas, much good farming land, a few towns – large by English standards – but small by any others, and dozens of modest market centres serving a local purpose though not noticeably significant in a wider sense. The people were still largely agricultural by interest and pursuit. More than three quarters of them lived and worked on the land and depended on it for their subsistence; and even the remainder, who inhabited the towns and made a living through crafts and trade, were mainly dependent on home-produced supplies of food and drink, and completely so for the raw materials of their business. London, both in its size and sophistication was well ahead of all the other cities in the country, but already it was clear that some ports, Bristol and Southampton for example, were developing rapidly, and some county towns like Norwich, Leicester, Exeter and Gloucester, assuming an administrative and social role in addition to their market functions. All the same, even in the towns, the agricultural foundations of the country were abundantly clear, in the nature of the goods being bought, sold and made, the way in which so many essentially urban people combined husbandry with other occupations, and the chequerboard pattern of town plans, in which houses, shops, and public buildings were interspersed with orchards, paddocks and small gardens where livestock could be kept, and herbs and vegetables grown.

The structure of this mainly agricultural society was no longer as simple as it had been in the early Middle Ages. The feudal pyramid, with the king at its apex, and easily recognisable ranks of interdependent classes fanning out to a wide base of labouring poor, had been distorted by the intrusion of completely independent elements such as the urban middle classes, and fatally weakened as the existing scheme of rights and duties was replaced by exclusively monetary contracts and relationships. This process of undermining had been encouraged by the very people who should have been interested in maintaining the status quo; for baronial and ecclesiastical landowners, while overtly subscribing to conservative measures such as the Statute of Labourers,[1] were at the same time inveigling workers away from their rightful masters with promises of wage rewards: or leasing out property in return for rents as opposed to military or other services. Thus it was a changing society, shot with uneasiness at lower levels where any departure from tradition seemed a threat to life itself, for which Henry had assumed responsibility, and it was to cope with the stresses occasioned by these changes that one aspect of his policy had to be shaped.

Social malaise, however, was only one of the problems facing the young king. Much more evident and serious were the consequences of the foreign and domestic wars the country had been involved in for the past 150 years or so. The Hundred Years' War, though only sustained actively for short periods at a time, had nevertheless been expensive in terms of money and men; and the Wars of the Roses, again a spasmodic conflict, had brought home to many parts of the country the devastating effects that the passage of an army – and usually it was more than one – could have on families and fortunes. For, whereas farmers were used to contending with the forces of nature while ploughing their fields and tending their animals, they were powerless to prevent pillaging, the destruction of livestock and crops, and damage to their homes at the hands of human agencies. Those involved in trade were similarly affected. While the Hundred Years' War had exacerbated the traditional rivalry between England and France and legalised the fighting in the Channel that went on anyway between the fishermen of both countries, it had also closed French markets to English goods, and disturbed

---

[1] Passed in 1351, to prevent workers leaving their feudal holdings in search of better conditions and money wages elsewhere.

the even more important cross-Channel trade in wool and woollen cloth to Calais and the Low Countries. The Wars of the Roses likewise had disruptive effects on the activities of the foreign and English merchants who in peaceful times toured the country to visit fairs, and on farmers, craftsmen and trades-people dependent on regular visits to local markets for the sale of agricultural products, raw materials and manufactured goods. As nothing was sacred to baronial retainers and hired soldiers, the protection usually extended to users of the highways, fairs and markets was worthless, and rather than risk their lives and goods, people chose not to travel.

But even more deeply felt than the material losses resulting from civil war were the twin evils of disorder and lawlessness, the inevitable concomitants of a situation where the king's authority could not prevail against magnates determined to use their power to prevent the existing machinery of government from serving the cause of justice and the interests of the country as a whole. Non-combatants perforce reconciled themselves to the depredations of war, but it was harder for them to accept the losses and damage that ensued when powerful lords, taking advantage of the lack of governance, fought out private feuds with their neighbours or seized coveted property with impunity, since few dared to prosecute them, and even those who did, had little hope of success when the presence of liveried retainers in or near the courts would always be the determinant of the verdict. In 1485, England's new king rightly perceived that his first objective must be to restore popular faith in the legal system and to establish a belief in his own ability to make this work universally and equitably.

In spite of the fact that ever since the Norman Conquest English kings had held, or advanced claims to, lands in France, the country as a whole was not greatly concerned with the situation in Europe during the Middle Ages, except when this had some bearing on trade. Protected by their island position, and very much on the fringe of the known world anyway, English men got on with the business of farming their land or selling their goods, and paid little heed to foreigners unless the latter threatened their material well-being in any way. But by the closing years of the 15th century their insularity was less rigid than it had been, because during the previous 100 years in the intervals of peace, English merchants, instead of waiting for their foreign counterparts to come here to buy them, had been carrying their own goods not only to the Low Countries and France, but further afield to Spain and Italy; and not long after Henry Tudor's accession, John Cabot's expedition was to sail from Bristol in search of new lands with trade potential on the other side of the world.

Meanwhile in the wake of trade had followed ideas and information. Those who travelled in Europe brought back, along with foreign goods, knowledge of new fashions in dress, architecture and learning, and once instinctive distrust of the unfamiliar had been overcome, fired the curiosity

Calais: the Staple port in Europe for English wool.

of their fellow Englishmen to discover more about what was happening in other countries. Also, as a result of the exploratory voyages of the Portuguese to Africa and India, and Columbus's discovery of America, the commercial centre of Europe was shifting from the Mediterranean to the Atlantic, and the pre-eminence enjoyed by Italy throughout the Middle Ages was passing to Spain, Portugal and the Low Countries, whence it would ultimately come to England. To keep their gaze turned inward and to ignore the possibilities now opening up of gaining wealth and prestige would have been foolish, and untypical of hard-headed business men; and if there were any who did have doubts or fears, the king himself quickly revealed his own conviction that England's best interest lay in aligning herself with the rest of Europe and participating in the opportunities offered by contemporary developments there. Henry's willingness to protect the merchant classes at home and safeguard their interests abroad, while not devoid of self-seeking, nevertheless showed that he realised the future

John Cabot: sailed from Bristol in search of a north-west passage to Asia.

importance of trade to the country as a whole, as well as to the Crown in particular.

Of necessity Henry was parsimonious when it came to spending money, since the less he spent, the less dependent he had to be on his subjects for financial support; all the same, he was quick to realise the use of regal magnificence to inspire respect among his subjects and contemporary European princes, whose favourable opinion he considered vital to his own standing and continuing success. A child of the Middle Ages by upbringing and no believer in innovation for its own sake, Henry was neverthless very much in tune with the age, in wanting to surround himself with an aura of majesty that would set him at a distance from his subjects and endow all his actions with a special quality that in time might come to be accounted as infallible. To be efficient was not enough: the king had to be an omniscient and omnipotent benefactor as well; only thus could he hope to keep at bay his subjects' intense fear of a return to civil war and lack of governance, and give them confidence to acquiesce unquestioningly in his leadership and policies. To this end, the trappings of grandeur and the exercise of princely patronage were invaluable. So although with only a vestige of the open-handed largesse indulged in by contemporary Italian princes and the French kings, Henry encouraged foreign scholars to come to his court, commissioned foreign artists and craftsmen to work for him, established University professorships and fostered an embryonic tradition of English music in his own Chapel Royal.

So by the end of the 15th century, thanks to Henry's shrewd interpretation of the people's needs, England had embarked on a period of revival, with the traditional machinery of government now being made to work efficiently under the authority of a strong monarchy; and when Henry died in 1509, the whole country was convinced that continuing stability and progress were tied up with the Tudor succession. Thus, no prince could have ascended the throne with more in his favour than did Henry's son. Thanks to his father's care with money, Henry VIII inherited a fortune that should have been sufficient to ensure his independence for the duration of the reign. Lawlessness and disorder had been firmly suppressed, and all the departments of government – administrative, executive and judicial – were functioning smoothly and effectively. The economy was prospering, England's prestige abroad was high, and Englishmen's faith and hopes in the future were unalloyed.

2
And of Gloucestershire in Particular

Like the remainder of England at the end of the 15th century, Gloucestershire was still largely agricultural, its three different regions – the Forest of Dean, the Severn Vale and the Cotswold Hills – producing a wide range of products that enabled the county to be more or less self sufficient in basic necessities.

The Forest of Dean, which covered the area between the river Severn and the river Wye, was only sparsely populated, since it was a royal hunting ground and settlement was prohibited there; nevertheless there were scattered communities on its borders and even in the forest itself, as the foresters of Dean were a law unto themselves and claimed the right to dig for coal wherever they could find it, regardless of royal prohibitions. As well as coal, which was becoming more important as the domestic use of it increased, there were valuable iron deposits in the area, sought after since long before the Romans came to Britain: also supplies of timber which provided material for domestic and farm uses in Gloucestershire and as far afield as the Midlands, and was invaluable for ship-building in ports along the Severn – Bristol, Lydney, Newnham and Gloucester. The valley of the Severn, with its fertile soil and mild climate, was primarily a region of arable and dairy farms interspersed with orchards in the north, producing food supplies that satisfied the needs of the county, the Midlands, the Welsh borders and the London area. The Cotswold Hills were generally regarded as bleak and inhospitable, yet they provided excellent grazing grounds for the flocks of sheep that were the source of England's staple export during the Middle Ages, and had sheltered valleys cut by streams in the limestone escarpment, where quite large villages could exist and thrive.

The productivity of these three regions was made the more valuable because there were useful communications within the county that facilitated the movement of goods by water and by road, to local markets and to a wide hinterland as well. The Severn, still easily navigable as far as Shrewsbury, the Warwickshire Avon, the tributaries of the Thames, and the Thames itself – navigable as far as Lechlade – were all main highways of traffic out of and into the county. Roads following the river valleys, as well as those that crossed the hills leading westward into Wales, south-west towards Bristol and Devon, and eastward to Oxford, carried their quota of

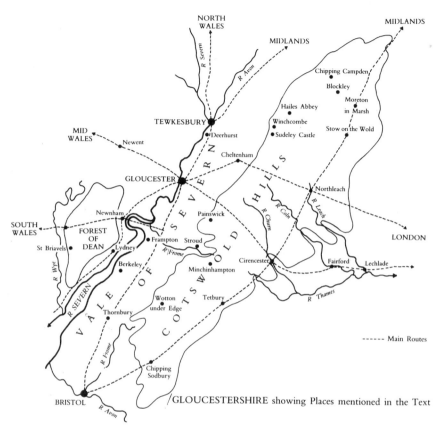

Map of Gloucestershire, showing its main regions.

pack-horses, wagons and droves of animals destined for markets outside the county. In fact, the routes that had made Gloucestershire accessible to invaders in the distant past, continued to be used by them after they became settlers here, and in time became a kind of economic framework, defining the main lines of the county's trade and business. The pattern of the routes also helped to explain the siting and development of towns in the county.

Although since Roman times, it was the south-eastern corner of England, with London at its centre, that was most densely populated, most prosperous and most progressive, Gloucestershire followed not far behind, and for an area situated at some distance from the capital, was unexpectedly advanced during the Middle Ages. The exchange of products between the different regions in the county had for centuries enabled its inhabitants to achieve a large measure of independence and self-sufficiency; but it was the early development of towns that explained a fairly steady increase in population, in communal activity and in wealth, which in turn led to social and cultural advances; and the establishment of the towns was largely due to the fact that so much of the land in Gloucestershire belonged to the Crown and the Church. Throughout the Middle Ages, Norman and Plantagenet kings, following the practice of their Anglo-Saxon predecessors and emulated in due course by their own tenants-in-chief, encouraged existing possibilities of trade, by channelling these into recognised markets where under the protection of a charter and in return for the payment of a yearly fee, local people and traders from elsewhere could safely conduct their business. The primary object of such a market was to provide an outlet for surplus products and a source of supplies, in respect of the overlord's estates in the area, but the benefit to the whole locality was quickly recognised. The grant of a charter cost nothing except to the townsfolk who paid for the privilege of having it, but the advantages both to the giver and the recipients| were numerous. The profits from buying and selling in the market, and rents from properties within the town, could more easily be realised than returns from an estate would have been, while the opportunity to live and work in an urban community freed from the demands for personal service or dues which were the concomitants of life in the country, was bound to appeal to any enterprising and ambitious worker.

So wherever a convergence of routes made it possible for traders of all kinds to assemble to do business, the towns had grown up. Some were at crossing places on rivers – Lechlade, Fairford and Tewkesbury for instance: some were natural focal points of ancient and mediaeval tracks like Wotton, Northleach, Stow on the Wold, Moreton in Marsh and Newent. Others benefited from the particular protection afforded by an abbey or a castle as at Cirencester, Winchcombe and Gloucester: or from the regular traffic up and down the river Severn, like Newnham, Lydney and Frampton. All, in due course, acquired the right to manage their own affairs free from any outside interference: to collect their own taxes and transmit them direct to the Royal Exchequer: to have a court to settle disputes between residents or arising out of business done in the town, and a council to make or enforce rules designed to ensure the safety and well being of the whole community. Town officials took themselves very seriously and expected a similar degree of respect from others. In Gloucester, no inhabitant of the town was 'to give words or unfitting language or any other unlawful demeaning to any of the Council.' In Tewkesbury, 'Every Lord's Day, both in the morning and afternoon . . . also upon all other solemn festivals and days appointed for fast and thanksgiving and yearly upon the day of Election of Office . . . it is ordered that everyone of the

The Court House at Stow on the Wold.

principal burgesses shall attend the Bailiffs to church in black cloth gown faced with velvet.' And not only on state occasions were the townsfolk expected to support their elected officers. Again at Tewkesbury, 'for better preservation of the peace . . . it is ordered that every person inhabiting within the town shall be ready to aid and assist all officers in doing their duty.'

Up to the end of the 15th century at least, there existed a large element of democracy in the way the town's affairs were handled, and considerable pride among the citizens in seeing that things were managed efficently. The borough records of Gloucester, Tewkesbury, Northleach and Tetbury are fuller and better preserved than some, but they are typical of all similar places. From them we can see the concern of town officials that the streets should be kept clean, safe and reasonably peaceful:

> Every householder shall from time to time provide that the pavements in the streets before his or her house be kept clean, and the dirt carried away, without sweeping the same into the gutters, and no swine or ducks to go in the open streets.
> Every substantial inhabitant living within this town . . . shall hang forth before their houses next the street, lanterns and candlelights . . .

there to burn from the beginning of night until 8 of the clock every
night except in the time of moonshining.

No man shall wear a long weapon, knife or sword, except he be an
officer of the town.

All possible precautions were to be taken against fire – a very real hazard
while there were still thatched roofs and timbered buildings: fire-fighting
equipment – buckets, ladders and hooks – was kept inside churches and it
was ordered that

No manner of person shall set fire wilfully in any chimney within his
house with the intension to make the same clean thereby, nor shall
negligently suffer his chimney to take fire to the danger of his
neighbours.

At market times special regulations were enforced. For the sake of fair
dealing and of hygiene, particular places were appointed for the buying and
selling of specified goods, the disposal of rubbish, and cleaning of vessels
and materials. At Tetbury there were two market houses appropriated to
distinct uses – one for cheese and bacon, the other for wool and yarn. At
Gloucester, 'no manner of cloth, woollen nor linen . . . to be sold, except
within the Boothall.' Again at Gloucester 'No one is to wash any clothes,
caps or any other thing at the place where the brewers get their water in the
Severn': and 'No one is to wash tubs, ale barrels or other filthy vessels at the
High Cross' (source of the town's water supply): and at Tewkesbury 'No
fishmongers to empty or wash down their stinking water, blood or filth
into the street or gutters.' The townsfolk were always anxious to exclude
from the privileges of the market anyone who was not a resident. Although
they were eager to collect dues from strangers for setting up stalls in the
market and for carrying goods into or out of the town, they neverthless
imposed certain restrictions on their coming and going, insisting that they
stayed with accredited hosts for strictly limited periods only, conducted all
their business in front of witnesses, and confined their dealings to certain
kinds of goods.

For the most part, business in the regular weekly markets consisted of an
exchange of agricultural products between farmers, the purchase of raw
materials (e.g. wool and skins) by town craftsmen, and the sale by the latter
of manufactured goods not easily obtainable in rural areas – boots, shoes,
saddlery and tools. But the existing contacts with areas outside the county
and the possibility of traders from elsewhere being interested in some of the
goods available locally, led to many of the towns seeking and obtaining
from the king the additional privilege of holding fairs each year, usually in
association with the feast day of the patronal saint of the parish church. A
fair lasted several days, as compared with the one-day weekly markets, and

The High Cross at Gloucester.

was carefully calendared to dovetail with similar events in other towns, so that merchants wanting to visit more than one had time to travel between the relevant places. (A charter grant always specified that a new fair must not be 'injurious' to any other in the neighbourhood). Where towns could offer local specialities in the way of foodstuffs, raw materials or manufactures, they concentrated on these, so in some places the main feature of the fairs came to be the strong, white wool of the Cotswold sheep that was so much in demand for the making of cloth in the Low Countries and Italy. It was this attraction that between the 12th and 15th centuries brought vast numbers of foreign merchants to the Cotswolds intent on buying up the best of the spring and autumn clips as well as fleeces, and in the sure knowledge that the quality of their purchases would be good. The Cotswold towns near the grazing grounds of the flocks belonging to the abbeys of Westminster, Gloucester, Tewkesbury, Evesham and Winchcombe – e.g. Chipping Campden, Northleach, Moreton-in-Marsh, Stow on the Wold and Fairford became famous for their fairs. 'Campden was a place of considerable importance when it was a most crowded mart for wool and the

Northleach: commemorative brass of Robert Serche (1501).

residence of the most opulent merchants who exported it to Flanders'.

The sale of the wool brought wealth and outstanding prosperity to Gloucestershire, and both contemporary and lasting fame to the men involved in it. Through their business correspondence, local benefactions and memorials in parish churches, the names of William Syger and William Grevel of Chipping Campden, Robert Serche and William Midwinter of Northleach, John and Edmund Tame of Fairford and Thomas Arnold of Cirencester as much today as in their own time, are associated with Cotswold wool and what could be achieved by means of it. But the trade had another aspect of importance to Gloucestershire as a whole. Since it was foreign merchants in person, or English agents employed by them, who attended the fairs, they came from London, Southampton and Bristol with foreign goods as well as money in hand, and carrying also the latest news, so that people in the county were brought into touch with developments and events in the capital and overseas. To judge by the correspondence of the Cely and Stonor families in England, and that of Francesco Datini from Italy, the dealers in wool were quite friendly with the men who sold and handled it at the fairs, relying on their advice, exchanging gifts with them, and seeking information about local affairs from them – even to the names of eligible marriage partners. Here was a factor then, that drew Gloucestershire into the main stream of national and international events.

The 15th century though, brought a change in the nature and direction of trade in Gloucestershire towns and the county generally. Disturbances on the continent and in particular the Hundred Years' War, interrupted the direct passage of wool from England to the staple port at Calais and the Low Countries; also both business men and government officials were coming to realise that the profits derived from the sale of raw wool were merely a fraction of what might be made from the sale of woollen cloth, especially if this was carried abroad by English traders and sold in the countries where it was wanted. So, by the end of the century there was a visible shift in trade, away from wool to woollen cloth, some destined for London, whence it was taken to the Low Countries and Germany, and some for France and Italy, in which case it was shipped from Southampton and Bristol. Local wool was still needed to supply the cloth manufacturers, but the latter tended to buy their raw materials as and when business demanded, consequently the seasonal importance of the wool fairs and their associated venues declined. Instead, a new significance attached itself to the places engaged in cloth manufacture – Cirencester, Painswick, Stroud, Uley, Dursley and Minchinhampton, where there was a plentiful supply of water for dyeing and fulling. The Tames who started as farmers and became wool merchants, continued their successful advance as clothiers, and remained prominent; but other families, made famous by the part they had played in the wool trade, were superseded by up and coming clothiers – the

The High Street, Chipping Campden: a great wool-market.

Gardners and the Webbs of Painswick, John Fortey and William Prelatte of Cirencester and John Townsend of Lechlade. In the 14th and early 15th centuries, it was the wool trade and the homes of the wool merchants that had established what appeared to be a high and enviable standard of living. By the end of the 15th century it was the turn of the clothiers: 'The seats of the clothiers present a scene of comfort and opulence not often to be paralleled.'

In due course we shall examine in greater detail the character of life in these towns, where thanks to the privileges bestowed by charters, men were free to make a living in their own chosen ways and to enjoy the profits of their labour without interference. Here it is sufficient to notice that by the closing years of the 15th century the towns had established themselves as centres of wealth and independence, as examples of success and self-sufficiency, and as spearheads of social and cultural advance. Already townsfolk were regarded with mingled admiration and envy by those who could not achieve their status and opportunities, and a gap was beginning to appear between sophisticated urban standards and outlook, and simpler rural ways. Although they still necessarily retained vital links with the countryside, the townsmen were anxious to emphasise how far they had moved away from their rustic forebears, and by placing themselves outside the framework of feudalism, which had to be totally comprehensive to retain its strength, they helped to hasten the end of the system.

By comparison with the towns, changes in the countryside came slowly and imperceptibly, and without seriously disturbing the manorial system that had been established at the time of the Norman Conquest. The arrangement whereby all land, save that reserved to the Crown, had been allocated to lay and ecclesiastical tenants-in-chief (who in turn sub-divided and sub-let their holdings) was originally designed to ensure adequate military aid for the kings when they needed it, but by the end of the 15th century the holding and use of land by tenants-in-chief had become divorced from military service, and was based instead on a monetary return. However, the division of holdings into manors and the responsibility of manorial lords for the management of their estates and the welfare of their dependent tenants remained. The manor courts still met regularly, under the lord or his steward, to decide on the basic pattern of farm practice in the demesne and tenant holdings: to ensure that everyone conformed with these arrangements: to record the payment of dues and changes in tenancies: and to deal with disputes and misdemeanours.

But since the 11th century two fundamental and significant changes had taken place in the country areas, and by the 15th century the results of these were visible. Whereas originally, a large proportion of the manorial tenants had rendered personal service and payments in kind to their overlord, this kind of subserviency had disappeared and the return for the use of land now took the form of money rents. Here and there, for another century at least, payments in kind continued, but these tended to be merely tokens – a capon at Christmas, a dozen eggs at Easter, a rose, some honey or spice – as was also the performance of personal services. In Gloucestershire, as elsewhere, one reason for the emancipation of tenants from a menial status was the outbreak of the Black Death in the 14th century which had carried off at least a half of the population, leaving the survivors in a strong position to bargain for improved tenancy agreements with their manorial lords. It must be noted too, that because of favourable farming conditions in the county, and the absence of over-powerful and demanding landowners, except when dogged by ill-luck or inefficiency, the dependent classes in Gloucestershire were not markedly down-trodden or hardly treated, which left them with enough resilience to survive natural hazards like bad harvests, and to exploit opportunities for bettering themselves. As we shall see, well before the enclosure movement became generally widespread, quite small tenant farmers here had made moves to consolidate their strip holdings in the village fields, and to rent, even if not to buy, more land for their own use.

The second change noticeable in the Gloucestershire countryside was a different attitude among landowners towards the management of their estates. Whereas in the 11th and 12th centuries, their primary and almost sole aim had been to ensure subsistence for their households and the means to fulfil their military obligations to the king, by the 15th century, a large

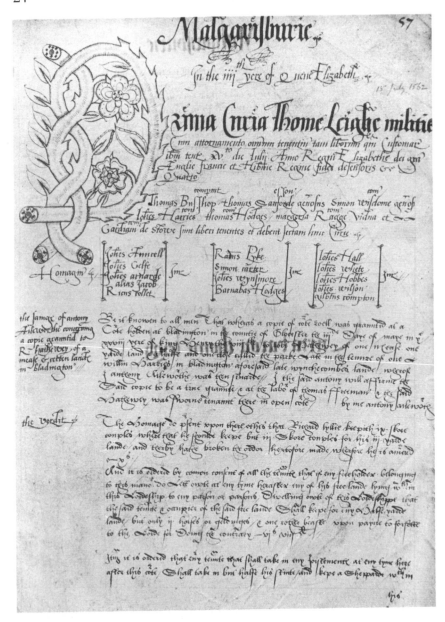

A page from the Manorial Roll of Maugersbury (1562).

number had come to regard their estates as a business proposition and were running them in such a way as to meet the expense of an increasingly comfortable standard of living for themselves and their families. Instead of following rigid and undeviating practices, manorial policy was now markedly flexible, and determined not by custom and precedent, but according to market demands for particular products, fluctuations in prices, and any current opportunities. Tenancies which fell vacant or were due for renewal were re negotiated on up-to-date terms: parts of the estate and even the demesne land were either leased or kept in the lord's hand, and the proportion of arable to pasture varied, according to which move promised to be most profitable at any particular time. One reason for this more business-like outlook may have been that a new type of landowner was appearing during the later Middle Ages, an incursor from the ranks of successful merchants and professional men in the towns, sometimes ignorant of, and certainly indifferent to, the demands of custom where land was concerned, and intent on running his newly-acquired estates as he would have done his previous undertakings. But it is also true that many owners whose lands had been handed down through generations (e.g. the Cliffords, Kingscotes, Guises and Tracys) were just as enlightened and enterprising as any of the newcomers, and succeeded in keeping up-to-date with farming practices and making profits that enabled them to improve and modernize their homes, dress fashionably, arrange good marriages for their children, and entertain – not extravagantly – but nevertheless on an impressive scale. The Tracys of Toddington, by concentrating on sheep rearing and very careful management of their estates, achieved a reputation for good husbandry and stable fortunes; while it was reported of Anthony Kingscote of Kingscote:

> It may be said of this gentleman and of his family . . . that he and his lineall ancestors have continued in this little manor nowe about 500 yeares, never attainted nor dwelling out of it elsewhere; nor hath the tide of his estate higher or lower, flowed or ebbed in better or worse condition; but like a fixed starre in his firmament, to have remained without motion in this little orbe, without any remarkable change.*

The towns and countryside in Gloucestershire suffered less than some areas from political disturbances during the Middle Ages and the Wars of the Roses in the 15th century. This was partly because, except for the Berkeleys – who owned much land and controlled the fate of many people in the south of the county – there were no other families with such a wide influence. On the whole, Berkeley patronage brought more good than evil in its train, though doubtless there were some among the family dependents

* Smith, *Lives of the Berkeleys.*

Berkeley Castle: stronghold and family home of the Berkeleys.

who deplored their feud with the Lisle family which lasted for 172 years and was pursued relentlessly by both sides, the legal actions involved paling into insignificance beside the looting and fighting that went on at the same time. The Marcher lords, Clare and Mortimer, owned manors in Gloucestershire which they used as staging posts en route to and from Wales, yet they do not seem to have attracted much of a following locally; while the rivalry between the Beauchamps and the Despensers, whose members had married into Gloucestershire families to secure land, was fought out at governmental rather than local level, and only affected the situation here, when estates became forfeit and changed hands.

Thus it had been possible for town and country folk alike, to detach themselves from politics to quite a large extent. Now and again, of their own accord, individuals did commit themselves to one loyalty or another, but with such mixed fortunes as to offer little encouragement to others to follow suit. In 1465, Ralph le Boteler, the owner of Sudeley Castle and Lord Treasurer of the country under Henry VI, 'was always for the Lancastrian line; but Edward IV attaining the Crown, he (le Boteler) was apprehended at Sudeley and brought prisoner to London.' He did at least escape with his life, unlike John Tiptoft, lord of the manor of Abbenhall, who served Edward IV 'but was then beheaded by the command of the great Nevil, Earl of Warwick, commonly called the Make-King, who in this year (1470) had restored Henry VI.' In the confusion of the Wars of the Roses, commitment to either side could and did prove hazardous, but even judicious neutrality occasionally failed to secure immunity from harm. The people of Tewkesbury, who had taken no part in the Lancastrian-Yorkist struggle before, were the passive victims of the battle that was fought there in 1474 between Margaret of Anjou and Edward of York, and it took them some time to recover from the slaughter of Lancastrians that made their rivers and streets run with blood and desecrated even the abbey itself.

Still, despite the sufferings of individual places and people, Gloucestershire escaped the worst of the vicissitudes that disturbed the central government during the reigns of Henry VI and Edward IV, and after the accession of Henry VII quickly returned to a state of stability where local government and affairs were concerned. However troubled the times, the manorial courts continued to meet and deal with petty local misdemeanours along with agricultural matters. Under a strong king there was nothing to prevent the shire courts assembling each month to deal with more serious crimes, and in special sessions when the Assize Judges arrived to take cognizance of cases involving serious breaches of the King's Peace. Elected constables were responsible at local level for the apprehension of criminals and their presentment for trial: Crown-appointed sheriffs for the handling of all business connected with the shire court. In particular circumstances, the king might appoint Justices of the Peace to deal with specific

Sudeley Castle: visited by Queen Elizabeth I.

administrative or judicial problems, but as yet the latter were not the 'Jack-of-all-Trades' they were to become under Elizabeth I. For the moment, local government continued as in the past, virtually isolated from the central government (except when the Assizes brought the suitors and officials of the shire court into contact with the royal judges) but none the less efficiently conducted, by local people with an understanding of local circumstances and local needs. Demands for taxes came as a reminder of the needs of the king, the periodic election of members of Parliament (2 from the county as a whole, and 2 each from the boroughs of Tewkesbury, Gloucester, Bristol) as a reminder of Gloucestershire's stake in central government; but the links that were to draw the whole county under the close scrutiny of the Royal Council and ministers by the end of the 16th century, had yet to be forged.

3
The Church and The Reformation

'Bare Ruined Choirs . . .'

The saying 'as sure as God's in Gloucestershire' was probably just an oft repeated piece of mediaeval alliteration and not a comment on the large number of religious foundations that there were in the county at that time; all the same, it was natural that it should have sprung to people's lips, since during the Middle Ages about a third of the land in Gloucestershire belonged to the church. Tewkesbury, Cirencester, Gloucester, Bristol, Winchcombe and Hailes all had large well-known abbeys with extensive estates scattered throughout the county and beyond; the wool towns – Chipping Campden, Northleach, Lechlade and Fairford for example – had churches that resembled small cathedrals, with high roofs, aisled naves, side chapels and magnificent tombs; and all but the smallest villages had gem-like parish churches, built in local stone by local masons whose signatures were the decorative carvings round doors and windows, intricate capitals and roof bosses, and the humorous grotesques of gargoyles and corbels.

The parish churches in villages and towns were largely the responsibility and very much the pride of their congregations, whose regular contributions maintained the fabric and roof of the nave (the priest was responsible for the upkeep of the chancel) and whose benefactions and financial bequests financed such additions as columned aisles, chapels, statues and stained glass windows. As yet the Christian Church was synonymous with society in so far as everyone was expected to subscribe to its practices and beliefs or else face the possibility of excommunication and subsequent ostracism by family and friends, a prospect dire enough to keep all but the most hardened sinners in the paths of righteousness. The priests, appointed by the Bishop of Worcester (or by abbots if a parish church was under monastic patronage) varied greatly in character and ability, being either learned scholars or little better educated than their congregations, zealous in pursuit of their duties or equally so in the avoidance of them. They were entitled to tithes (a tenth of the produce or income of each of their parishioners) which were expected to satisfy their personal needs and leave enough in hand for charitable uses; they were not supposed to expect or accept anything more, but by the 15th century, a great number of incumbents either from genuine need or cupidity, charged fees for conducting services of baptism, marriage or burial, for hearing confession

Lechlade Church: resembling a small cathedral.

and even for non-professional help such as reading or writing a letter. Since it was generally believed that life on earth was merely a brief preliminary to what might be a long and blissful after-life, provided that the teachings of the church were obeyed, the priest had a powerful hold over his flock, few of whom demurred when required to pay for essential spiritual aids, or reminded of the immorality of holding on to undue profits made in trade or business.

Natural focal points in the locality, and with their daily services and seasonal celebration of Saints' Days and festivals providing the only breaks in an otherwise unvarying existence, the parish churches were very much a part of the every-day life of the people. By contrast, the monasteries were detached from the world, in so far as their inmates were bound by vows that should have made them indifferent to all material considerations. The chief orders of monks – Benedictine and Cistercian – were well represented in Gloucestershire, as were also the Military Order of Knights Templar, the Friars and the Augustinian Canons. The layout of monastic buildings varied in detail according to the daily routine and requirements of the particular orders, but all included a large church with aisles and side chapels for processional and celebratory purposes, a library, a chapter-house, domestic and living quarters for the inmates, and separate, more sumptuous accommodation for the head of the community. The land for the buildings had usually been given in the first place by kings or magnates, and dependent estates subsequently added as a result of gifts and legacies which were either pious expressions of gratitude for outstanding good fortune – a recovery from illness, a safe return from war, – or else a hopeful investment to ensure a rewarding after-life. Though forbidden as individuals to accept or own any worldly goods, members of Regular orders were allowed to add to the possessions of their community, so it was possible for the establishment to become extremely well-endowed with land, and for the church – which was the centre of all communal activites – to be richly furnished with jewelled lamps and statues, fine cloths and tapestries, stained glass windows, candlesticks, crosses and vessels of gold and silver.

By the 15th century, the monastic institutions in Gloucestershire were very considerable in size. The Friars and Canons, though mainly concerned with pastoral work in the towns, nevertheless had their houses and lands from which they derived revenues, both groups having important establishments in Bristol, Gloucester and Cirencester. The estates of the Cistercian houses – at Kingswood, Flaxley and Hailes – were kept very closely under control, either directly from the mother house, or else from granges in charge of monastic stewards. Even the animals on Cistercian estates were expected to conform to the strict rules of the order. 'Pig styes can be two or even three leagues from a grange, but pigs though they can wander by day, must return to the styes at night.' The Knights Templar, bound by strict

A monastic barn at Great Barrington.

orders themselves, while leasing some of their lands to lay farmers, were very assiduous in exacting the agreed terms of tenancies from the lessees – payments in kind, labour and carrying services. The Benedictines – at Bristol, Gloucester, Tewkesbury and Winchcombe – were ready not only to lease their lands but also to use laymen as stewards, which explains why – at the dissolution – some of the latter were so knowledgeable about which monastic estates were worth procuring for themselves.

As pioneers in sheep-rearing on a large scale, the Benedictines and Cistercians were responsible for giving the first impetus to the wool trade in Gloucestershire. Not only did the abbeys own huge grazing grounds on the hills; at busy times the size of their flocks necessitated the employment of extra labour for driving the sheep to places where they were to be dipped and sheared, and for collecting the sheared wool and fleeces. So vast were these operations that they became almost ritualistic, with all other work in the neighbourhood being suspended while the men coped with the influx of sheep and the women catered for the needs of the workers. Contemporary accounts record the amounts paid out on these occasions for wages and victuals, which seem trifling (perhaps £4 or £5 in all) in view of the numbers of sheep handled – often 3,000 or 4,000 at a time. It was for the storage of the wool that special barns had to be built, such as that of Lanthony Priory at Barrington, of Hailes at Farmcote, of Tewkesbury at Stanway and of Worcester at Bibury, where the famous Arlington Row (now a group of separate cottages) was once a single building, and the land in front of it named the Rack Isle, since it was here that the wool was hung out to dry before being stored.

Even more important than their economic role in the county was the social significance of the monasteries, since from the time of their establishment they had afforded shelter and hospitality to travellers, charity to local paupers and vagrants, medical aid to the sick, and education to the young, whether these were destined for the church or not. Establishments on main highways – at Cirencester, Gloucester and Tewkesbury for instance – were never without visitors: those in the vicinity of royal manors or places of administrative importance were regular stopping places for sovereigns or royal officials: while others had their special inherent attractions, saintly images and shrines, and – at Hailes and Gloucester – the Blood of Hailes and the tomb of Edward II, both objectives of pilgrimages. The former, reputed to be some drops of Holy Blood contained in a phial, was accounted miraculous in so far as it was only visible to those who had been absolved of all their sins, to attain which state, pilgrims were prepared to reward lavishly the monks who guarded the relic. Hugh Latimer, Bishop of Worcester, commented in the 1530's: 'I dwell within half a mile of the Fosseway and you would wonder to see how they come by flocks out of the west country to many images, but chiefly to the Blood of Hailes.' The tomb of Edward II at Gloucester had begun to attract attention within a short while of the king's burial there, and in spite of his disastrous reign and his unpopularity during the course of it, the miracles reported by pilgrims to the tomb almost achieved canonisation for Edward, and certainly added considerably to the revenue of the abbey.

The passage of travellers, of pilgrims to the shrines, and of officials going to and fro on monastic business meant that there was always movement and human interest in the vicinity of the monasteries. The arrival of distinguished visitors, fashionably dressed and with servants in attendance, or the departure of the abbot – also with a retinue – bound for another abbey or the king's court in London, provided subjects for gossip and speculation to the people in the locality, as well as extra work for blacksmiths, saddlers and carters. Where the abbey served as a parish church – as at Tewkesbury, or administered a church for the parish – as at Cirencester, there were regular opportunities to see the interior of the building, watch the processions, hear the singing of the monastic choir, and thus get caught up in and (temporarily) become part of the life of the establishment. Finally, there was a definite link between the monasteries and the upper ranks of local society. Younger sons, destined for a career in the church, might begin

The nave of Tewkesbury Abbey: saved from dissolution for the sum of £473.

their training at a monastic school and old men, anxious to spend their last days free of worldly cares, could become corrodians, enjoying their own rooms and attendance, regular meals and medical care if sick; also as has been said, laymen were sometimes asked for legal advice or practical help in running monastic estates, so that in spite of their essential commitment to unworldliness, the monks had neverthless quite close links with local communities and local society. 'The religious houses were accepted as long-standing members of local society; people sponged upon them, quarrelled with them in endless lawsuits, hobnobbed with them and distracted them from the life of religion.'*

The changes in religion which were introduced in the 1530's as a result of Henry VIII's decision to divorce Katherine of Aragon and marry Anne Boleyn did not constitute as sharp a break with the past, nor surprise people as much as might be expected. Powerful though he had made himself and indispensable as he was – in popular estimation – to the continued well being of the country, Henry could not have been so successful in his plans if the times had not been propitious and the more influential of his subjects in a mood to consider and accept new practices and new values where religion was concerned. In Gloucestershire the ground had been prepared for the Reformation over a century earlier, when the teaching of John Wycliffe had taken a firm hold in the county. Lollard ideas had been disseminated largely from Bristol where a number of craftsmen and traders had links with London and the Midlands, by means of which they freely and easily obtained heretical literature. So keen were they to spread their opinions that 'Books were throwen in the strete and left at mennes dores by nyghte, that where they durst not offer their poysen to sell, they would of their charitie poysen men for nought.' But such crusading efforts would not have been effective had there not been receptive minds ready to be converted to a new point of view; and Lollard attacks on the shortcomings of the clergy, and the greed and worldliness of the Church in general, found many sympathisers. Because of its political implications (some of the upper classes espoused Lollardy and were suspected of having designs on the state as well as the Church) the movement was firmly repressed but not effectively destroyed, so its influence lingered on to be fanned into flame again in the early 16th century when Lutheran ideas of religious reform began to spread to England from Germany, and Tyndale's version of the New Testament came into circulation here (from 1526 onwards).

William Tyndale constituted a link with Lollardy in so far as his outlook and views, though essentially a response to contemporary circumstances, closely resembled those of the earlier 'heretics' and showed the extent to which the latter had created a receptive climate for 16th century ideas of

* Dickens: *The Reformation in England.*

William Tyndale, a Gloucestershire reformer.

reform. He was born in Gloucestershire about 1495, was educated at Oxford and then became a tutor in the household of Sir John Walsh at Little Sodbury. While there he fell foul of the local clergy for some outspoken public speeches, and this may have intensified his opposition to them and encouraged his idea of producing a version of the New Testament in English. In all probability he would have seen a Lollard Bible, copies of which were still circulating in the early 16th century, and been strengthened by this in his belief that the Scriptures should and must be translated into the vernacular and made easily available to all sincerely religious persons, one of the principles of the Lutherans of his own time. The vocabulary used in his translation also made clear the other views which Tyndale shared with the German reformers – disapproval of the hierarchy of the clergy, of superstitious practices, and of the undisputed and undisputable power of the Church; while his marginal notes revealed even more clearly his distrust of the Papacy and the jealous way in which churchmen regarded the Scriptures and indeed anything to do with religion, as their particular prerogative.

Copies of Tyndale's *New Testament* fell into eager hands when they reached England (like Lollard works, this was published in the Low Countries and subsidised by English cloth merchants abroad), for by the

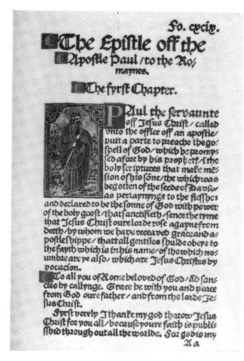

A page from Tyndale's New Testament in English.

early 16th century the spread of education especially among the upper and middle classes was encouraging a more independent and critical outlook, anti-clerical and anti-papal in its tendencies. Men who were learning to think for themselves naturally resented any restrictions such as the Church was accustomed to place on sources of information, just when the New Learning – spreading from Italy and made widely available because of printing – was introducing an exciting range of subjects hitherto unknown to the layman. Tyndale's criticism of the worldliness of the clergy and the Papacy also found a sympathetic hearing among successful business men whose concern with money matters was condemned by the Church, and whose profits were expected to be devoted to charity or ecclesiastical endowments; whereas many of those who – by vocation – had disavowed material considerations and embraced poverty, were in fact enjoying the fruits of this world and – because of their calling – an exemption from any of the payments and penalties that laymen automatically incurred.

Simon Fish, one of those responsible for distributing Tyndale's *New Testament* in England, was also the compiler of the *Supplication of the Beggars*, presented to Henry VIII in 1529, and purporting to summarise the complaints of ordinary people against the demands and blackmailing tactics of avaricious clergy. 'Even the poor tithe-paying housewife must account for every tenth egg, or be taken as a heretic.' The king received the pamphlet with interest and is said to have carried it about with him for some time – perhaps not so much because he believed it to be a comprehensive report on the state of the Church in England and of popular attitudes towards it, as because he could see in it a potential weapon for his own use, should he have to face opposition from the clergy in his efforts to obtain a divorce from Katherine of Aragon.

Henry moved carefully towards the point where his Supremacy over the Church in England was established by act of Parliament and accepted by the clergy in Convocation, thus making it possible for him to proceed exactly as *he* wished in respect of his marriages and the conduct of church affairs generally. Thanks to the *Supplication of the Beggars*, he was already acquainted with certain sections of public opinion and felt reasonably confident that measures designed to reform the clergy, restrict payments to the Church and end the power of the Pope to interfere in England, would not only be passed by Parliament but also accepted by the majority, if not all, of his subjects; and since the monasteries had been included in the general criticism levelled at the Church, he expected that even their destruction could be carried out without serious opposition.

Although they came after the other reform measures, it was the acts dissolving the smaller monastic houses in 1536 and the larger ones in 1538 that had the most marked effect at first, especially in Gloucestershire, where so much of the land had been in monastic hands. In the case of the smaller houses, worth less than £200 a year, like Flaxley, and friaries at Bristol and Gloucester, the monks were persuaded to agree to the 'voluntary surrender' of their houses, and accepted either transfer to larger establishments or absolution from their vows to enable them to seek other work. Their houses, lands and material possessions automatically came under the jurisdiction of Henry's Court of Augmentations set up to deal with this situation. The larger houses presented a more difficult problem, not so much because of the greater number of monks in them, but because – on various grounds – there was a passive, but quite effective reluctance to accept what must surely by then have seemed the inevitable, namely Henry's assertion of authority over the monks, and the assumption of their wealth and possessions for his own needs.

The arguments, mainly economic and administrative, that had been used to bring about the surrender of the smaller houses, were not so easily applied to the larger ones, where affairs may have fluctuated between solvent stability and near bankruptcy, but on the whole were reasonably prosperous and well-managed. It was reported of Hailes for instance, on the eve of the dissolution:

Lechlade: St John's Bridge, a monastic responsibility.

> The father had his house so well-furnished with jewels, plate, stuff, corn, cattle and the woods also so well saved as though he had looked for no alteration of his house.

Some, when faced with questions put by the Commissioners appointed by Thomas Cromwell, (Henry's Vicar-General in respect of church affairs) pleaded their usefulness to the local community. The next to last abbot of Winchcombe, Richard Kidderminster had, it was claimed, 'by his encouragement of virtue and good letters . . . made the monastery flourish so much that it was equal to a little university.' The monks of Deerhurst and Lechlade pointed out the importance of their work in maintaining the roads and bridges in the vicinity; and every house might have claimed, though it did not necessarily do so, that in its time it had been responsible for clearing, draining and fencing its lands and providing employment. Tewkesbury had long afforded hospitality to passing travellers and also supplied alms regularly to pay for clothing, feeding and educating a number of poor scholars. The abbot of Kingswood tried a different approach. In order to ingratiate himself with Cromwell, he sent a little book written in support of the Royal Supremacy begging him' to open the eye of pity to me and the religious men of this house who have no succour except in your evangelical charity.'

The commissioners were specifically appointed (and ordered?) to find plausible reasons for the dissolution. They were laymen, and therefore

Winchcombe: the George Inn, a stopping place for pilgrims to Hailes Abbey.

unsympathetic and unimaginative where the vocation and work of the monks were concerned. Some of them had a vested interest in the redistribution of the monastic estates; and all were inclined to be hasty in their judgments, to stress the undesirable aspects of what they found and overlook the better ones. On occasion they were helped by recalcitrant monks, only too ready to provide evidence against their superiors, like John Norwood at Winchcombe. The records of Tewkesbury abbey revealed that although the revenues of the house were adequate to its size, the abbot had so arranged matters that he had personal control of two-thirds of the money, and used it to secure an extravagant standard of living for himself. The monks of Gloucester profiteered from pilgrims visiting the tomb of Edward II, a superstitious practice it is true, though the funds had largely been used to rebuild part of the abbey church. But it was at Hailes that circumstances really played into the hands of the investigators, since the miracles claimed for the Blood of Hailes and the Papal Indulgence bestowed on all who 'gave alms to the worship of God and the Precious Blood of Hailes' epitomised the kind of superstitions that were incensing contemporary lay opinion. We have noticed Latimer's amazement at the number of pilgrims who regularly made their way to Hailes; and this was more than matched by the ardour of those who sought to discredit the practice: 'We have been boulting and sifting the Blood of Hailes all this forenoon, and verily it seems to be an unctuous gum and compound of many things.' The so-called miracle whereby the absolved sinner had been enabled to see the Blood, was explained away by the monks having 'changed the crystal before it from thick to thin, once the pilgrim had paid for as many masses as they pleased and at as great a price.' 'An horrid cheat' remarked a later commentator.

There was no sympathetic response in Gloucestershire to the Pilgrimage of Grace which was the result of the proposed dissolution of monasteries in the northern counties; nor, apart from verbal exchanges with Cromwell beforehand, was there any active opposition here to the arrival of the kings' men appointed to strip the establishments of gold and silver plate, furnishings and lead, before making them uninhabitable, lest any of the inmates should linger in the neighbourhood and try to return. As in many other areas, there were stories told of monastic treasures being removed and hidden before the despoilers could lay hands on them, but no great finds have ever been made to prove that such things actually happened. Undoubtedly some of the gold and silver plate and tapestries were removed, since these reappeared later among the furnishings of private

The ruins of Hailes Abbey.

Chavenage: the front view of the house.

houses, but most of the materially valuable and useful goods were carried off to the Royal Treasury. The buildings themselves were effectively damaged, the roofs removed, stained glass windows smashed (so that their lead framework could be retrieved), statues and altars defaced and thrown down, and perhaps most serious of all for posterity, most of the records, priceless manuscripts and books destroyed. At Cirencester, Winchcombe, Gloucester and Tewkesbury the abbey churches were allowed to remain since they were also the parish churches of these towns; in fact, the congregations had contributed regularly to repairs and additions to the naves and rightly felt that they had a vested interest in them. At Tewkesbury they raised £453 and presented it to the king to ensure that the church remained in their possession for parish use. For the rest, the cloisters, chapter houses and living quarters of the monks lapsed into roofless ruins, and became convenient quarries for local farmers who needed stones for walls and gateposts, or local builders erecting or embellishing country houses later in the century. At Wightfield Manor the stones of a chapel from Deerhurst Priory were incorporated into the walls and a whole Norman porch removed and reconstructed into a garden gateway; the tower of Toddington church was built of material from Hailes Abbey; the ruins of Horsley Priory were used as a quarry during the rebuilding of Chavenage.

The closing of the monasteries, however, had less devastating effects for their inmates than was once believed to be the case. The picture of hundreds of monks driven forth, homeless and without any means of subsistence, is now known to be misleading, as is also the claim that they added considerably to the already rising number of workless, and thus aggravated the contemporary problems of poverty and unemployment. In fact, whether with a foreknowledge of events or not, some abbeys had made provision for a number of their members in that the latter had been appointed to serve dependent churches, where they were now allowed to stay. After the dissolution of the smaller houses, many monks took advantage of the opportunity 'to exchange a monkish habit for the seemly garb of a secular priest'; and when the larger houses were closed, pensions were granted to the inmates (to be paid out of the funds of the Court of Augmentations) many of whom also took on parochial responsibilities. The abbot of Tewkesbury, John Wakeman, was appointed to be the first bishop of the new see of Gloucester, after the abbey of St. Peter had been transformed into a cathedral establishment in 1541, with some of the monks staying on to serve as cathedral clergy; monks, in the role of secular clergy, also continued to tend the churches at Cirencester and Tewkesbury. The abbots of Winchcombe and Hailes were given prebends at Gloucester and York respectively, but the abbot of Cirencester and the prior of Lantony retired from the church altogether and took up residence in country houses

Gloucester: the abbey of St Peter, turned into a cathedral in 1541.

(provided as part of their pensions) at Brockworth and Fairford. Of the ordinary monks, some obtained livings within the county (the abbots of Tewkesbury and Winchcombe) were particularly conscientious on behalf of their former brethren) and enjoyed their pensions and preferments until they died. Others were found parishes elsewhere, just as some monks from houses outside Gloucestershire, thanks to influence and patronage, were appointed here.

Clearly it would not be safe to generalise from these particular cases, and assume that all the monks were provided for, nor is it possible even to calculate the numbers of those that had an adequate subsistence as opposed to those that did not. Pensions varied from as little as £4 a year to over £15, and since – until inflation began to get worse in the 1550's – £5 a year would have provided adequate keep, the ex-monks cannot have been starving. The state conducted regular investigations, as far as it was able, into the fate of its pensioners, partly out of real concern and partly out of necessity caused by abuses e.g. the continued collection of money by friends after the death of the real pensioners. Until 1551, payments continued regularly, but after that – because of the rate of inflation – any pensions of over £10 a year were stopped. However, the official records prove that there was considerable concern shown for the dispossessed monks, and that though their lives may not have been as sheltered and straightforward as before, at least they were not entirely destitute.

However, it was not only the monks and their lands that were affected by Henry VIII's reform measures and the religious changes of subsequent reigns. Originally Henry did not intend to interfere with the doctrine or the practices of the Church in England (after all he had won his title of Defender of the Faith for supporting the Catholic Church against Lutheran attacks on it), nevertheless, in order to ensure the continuing support of those who favoured reform, he allowed Thomas Cromwell to introduce and enforce certain changes which he (Henry) believed were still consistent with the Church remaining Catholic in character, though headed by the King instead of the Pope. The direction of ecclesiastical dues into the Exchequer instead of to Rome, and the submission of the clergy to the royal will and the royal courts made little difference to the average layman; but the impact of the Cromwellian Injunctions designed to regulate the conduct of the clergy in the performance of their duties, necessarily repercussed on to their congregations. That the priests should cease to encourage or even countenance superstitious practices (so-called) – e.g. the hearing of Confessions, the saying of prayers for the dead, the reverencing of relics and burning of candles – cut the people off from the touchstones of their faith and left simple souls worried about the consequences of the non-fulfilment of customary observances. That the priests and parish officials should undertake the removal from the church of roods and rood screens, pictures, statues, altar hangings and missals deprived the congregations of familiar outward signs of their faith and left them to look helplessly at white-washed walls, unadorned aisles and bare altars. Finally the introduction of copies of the Bible in English into every church and the admonitions to the clergy to teach the members of their flock the Lord's Prayer and the Creed in English, and to preach a sermon to them at least once a quarter, introduced a new element into church services, not necessarily as welcome as contemporary

Fairford Church: Choir Stalls and Rood Screen.

reformers were wont to claim, for, whether intelligible or not, the Latin of the Mass and other services had at least been familiar, whereas the new English wording was not.

Not until more radical changes were introduced in Edward VI's reign, was there the violent iconoclasm that led to stained glass windows being smashed: stone altars wrenched from their settings: chantry chapels and sanctuaries destroyed: but already by the end of Henry's reign many of the rich furnishings and plate belonging to the parish churches had disappeared – hidden against future need, as were the altar stones of North Cerney and Northleach, and the churchyard cross at Ampney Crucis: taken for private use, or sold and the proceeds spent on repairs, 'charitable uses' (Newnham), 'the mendyng of the highe waye betwixte the said parishe and Huntley (Longhope) and 'the setting forth of soldeours in the king's majesty's warres' (Stanton). At the same time, church interiors were also changed by the introduction of lecterns to hold the Great Bible, a pulpit for the preacher, and benches or fixed pews for the congregation who were now expected to be intelligent participants in the service instead of mere spectators.

For the most part Gloucestershire people seem to have been content to go along with the changes ordained by both Henry VIII and Edward VI – the laity from ignorance or inclination, and the clergy from a desire to cling to their positions. Except in the towns where the more zealous reformers were to be found, reaction to official demands tended to be cautious though, and only the final innovations of Edward's reign – the introduction of a Prayer Book in English, the dissolution of the chantries, the substitution of wooden tables for stone altars – put an end (for the time being at any rate) to traditional attitudes and usages. As in the days of Lollardy, many ordinary folk became acquainted with the Scriptures through the availability of the English Bible, and accustomed to quoting them. As early as 1537 Edward Fox, bishop of Hereford, commented 'the lay people know the Scripture better than many of us'. Even when, in the closing years of his reign, Henry sensed a certain danger in the spread of a little learning among the masses and restricted the possession of English Bibles to churchmen and noble households, many copies continued in the hands of lesser folk. Robert Williams, a shepherd of Saintbury, wrote in one of his books: 'I bout thys boke when the Testament was obberagatyd (abrogated) that shepyerdes myght not rede jit. I pray God amende that blyndnes.' In justification of Henry's qualms it must be said that not every humble reader was as intelligent as Robert Williams, and some got things badly wrong, as for instance he who asserted: 'I know the law is for me to have children by adultery. I wolde wysshe Moses' law to be again.'

In responding to the demands of official policy, the clergy and their congregations largely kept pace with each other. In some cases lack of

Hugh Latimer, Bishop of Worcester.

education and discernment, and in most a desire to remain in office, prevented parish priests from becoming advocates of, or leaders in, particular policies. Here and there, an especially keen supporter of reformed ideas did appear – William Latimer of Saintbury and William Dingley of Stow on the Wold for instance; but there were places also where the zeal of the congregation outstripped that of their priest to fulfil the required of sermons and catechizing, and where the former introduced the practice of hiring their own preacher to fill the gap. This easy-going acquiescence of the majority in what was required of them, prevented any violent demonstrations in Gloucestershire over particular innovations (as for instance there were in Cornwall and East Anglia over the English Prayer Book) and it also explains why, even when there were upholders of reform in high places doing their best to hasten the process of change, they had little lasting influence.

Hugh Latimer, the first of these, bishop of Worcester from 1535 to 1539, came to office with a reputation for being 'a diligent and vigilant pastor', and a new broom dedicated to sweeping clean. We have already noticed his disapproval of pilgrimages; and in his episcopal office he made a point of condemning all superstitious practices and laying down strict rules for his subordinate clergy to follow, forbidding them 'to set aside preaching for any manner of observance in the church, or processions and other ceremonies,' or 'to discourage any lay person from the reading of good books.' John Wakeman, the abbot of Tewkesbury, who became first bishop of the new see of Gloucester, was less whole-hearted in his commitment to new practices, and though like Latimer he conducted regular visitations in the diocese and presided over the episcopal court where punishment was meted out to moral offenders, there was no marked persecution of those who failed to comply with official policy. That Wakeman's own attitude was a compromise between the new and the old is shown for instance in the continued use of traditional practices where penance was concerned – the saying of a set number of prayers before the altars of certain churches, and even as in the old days, the commutation for the sentence by money payments. Whether from lack of conviction or of courage, though he had benefited materially as a result of Henry's reform policy, Wakeman made certain that whichever way things went in the future, i.e. towards more extreme reform measures or back to true Catholicism, he would not have committed himself so completely to one course as to make it impossible for him to change to another.

John Hooper, third of the leaders of reform in Gloucestershire, was more extreme in his views than the other two. After the dissolution of the Blackfriars at Gloucester in 1538 he had spent the last years of Henry VIII's reign abroad in Switzerland, whence he returned totally committed to Protestant views and practices and uncompromising in his determination to remove from the church in England any remaining traces of Catholicism. Appointed to the see of Gloucester in 1550 and jointly with that of Worcester in 1552, Hooper was only too ready to go along with the policy designed by Edward VI and his ministers to complete – for spiritual reasons – the reforms that Henry VIII had initiated in pursuit of personal and political ends. Like Latimer, he opposed all superstitious practices and outward reminders of the Old Faith, and only under pressure agreed to wear episcopal robes for his own consecration. A deeply spiritual man, he believed that individuals were responsible for their own salvation and that it was the duty of the Church to help them in this, hence his desire to have removed from church buildings any physical barriers (i.e. rood screens, remote altars, separate chantry chapels) that might segregate the congregation from the priest in the course of a service. Hooper thought too, that a priest in his own life must afford a model worthy to be followed by members of his flock, who with the aid of regular preaching and catechizing should be encouraged to live up to his example. Small wonder then that the bishop was shocked (though not daunted) when his official visitations

uncovered widespread evidence of unfitness among the Gloucestershire
clergy. (He claimed that after a brief stay in Worcester, he was obliged to
return to Gloucestershire 'because of the negligence and ungodly behaviour
of the ministers there'.) During his short episcopate, 1550–1554, he was
tireless in his zeal for reform; he travelled all over the diocese, making
surprise descents on unwitting incumbents whom he subjected to searching
questionnaires and suspended from duty if their answers were unsatisfac-
tory. (Of the 311 clergy he examined, 168 could not repeat the Ten
Commandments, 39 did not know where the Lord's Prayer appeared in the
Bible, while 34 could not say who was its author). Hooper's austerity and
stern devotion to duty foreshadowed that of the later Puritans: but he was at
heart a humane man, very much aware of the plight of the poor, and critical
of greedy, unfeeling landlords and employers; and clearly his sympathy was
noted and appreciated: 'He was so adored by the people that they had him
for a prophet, nay they looked upon him as some deity.'

But however much Latimer and Hooper in turn might strive to instil
sound beliefs and practices into Gloucestershire congregations, they could
make little headway without the determined co-operation of parish priests;
and this they never got, since so many incumbents continued uneducated
and uncommitted, and no better ones presented themselves for ordination
while parochial means of subsistence remained meagre. Priests and
congregations followed in the wake of official policy at their own pace, and
by the end of Edward's VI's reign to all outward appearances were in line
with official requirements. That the innovations were not making a very
deep impression generally is borne out by the matter-of-fact way in which
church accounts record sums of money being spent first of all on the
installation of a chantry, an additional altar, or a statue, and then later the
removal or the destruction of the same piece of work; and it is also
significant that the very people who had revered Hooper also turned out to
see him burned at the stake during the Marian reaction to reform.
Nevertheless during the reigns of Henry and Edward there was a steady
move towards non-Catholic practices, and an essentially English liturgy:
and meanwhile outward reminders of the old form of religion disappeared
from parish churches just as monastic and chantry buildings had done
elsewhere.

Although there was a brief return to Catholicism under Mary
(1553–1558) it was Protestant influences and tendencies that determined the
style in which the parish churches were to go on and survive. Clearly there
was no systematic destruction and despoiling here, otherwise the glorious
windows of Fairford would not have remained intact, nor other examples
of mediaeval glass be still visible in the abbey churches at Gloucester and
Tewkesbury and in smaller churches such as Bledington, Buckland and
Edgeworth. Wall paintings too have survived at Hailes, Baunton and

Evenlode Church: the pre-Reformation Pulpit.

Oddington, and been rescued from under coats of whitewash at Kempsley: and a few rare pieces of embroidery, examples of that valuable mediaeval export Opus Anglicanum, in the form of copes and altar frontals at Buckland, Chipping Campden and Baunton. Pulpits were rare before the Reformation because occasional sermons were the least important part of church services, but Gloucestershire does have a few early examples, as at North Cerney, Colesbourne, Naunton and Evenlode. Of memorials, the best known are the brasses of the wool merchants at Northleach, Chipping Campden, Cirencester and Lechlade, of two priests at Blockley, and of knights at Dyrham and Deerhurst, all of them reflecting a certain pride in success, and carrying a wealth of detail of contemporary costume. In a different way, but no less remarkably, the stone monuments of the Despencers and Beauchamps at Tewkesbury, of Edward II and Abbots Serlo and Parker at Gloucester, of the Berkeleys and others at Coberley embody the greatness of these people as well as the skill of the mediaeval masons who carved their memorials.

Other pre-Reformation features were superseded or replaced. The chantry chapels lost their separate significance when the practice of saying prayers for the dead was forbidden, and were either claimed by the families of the founders and turned into private pews, or incorporated as aisles into the main body of the church, as at Longborough, Barnsley, Cirencester and Coberley. Porches often used as extensions of the church for services and the sealing of contracts, and which had their own altar niches where the poor could place candles (not being able to afford lights suitable for the high altar) became mere entrances after the Reformation, or in the case of Cirencester's magnificent three storeyed building, the Town Hall. The roods and rood screens, after the altars perhaps the most significant features of the mediaeval churches and therefore one of the main targets of the reformers' zeal, have almost all disappeared, but the carving of the arms of Henry VIII above the chancel arch at Cirencester where the rood screen would have been, is a reminder of how the royal will triumphed over centuries of popular beliefs and practices.

The ordinary people who perforce were a party to these changing circumstances, aware that along with the familiar ritual of the Latin Mass. the colourful interest of their church buildings was being extinguished, accepted whatever happened even if they did not altogether understand the significance of it. But they were too near their mediaeval past for their religious instincts to have changed fundamentally and they still needed insurance (and reassurance) and opportunities for beneficent gestures; so, forbidden to give money for candles to light the high altars and side chapels, or for priests to say prayers for their souls, they spent it instead on even more magnificent memorials than their ancestors if they belonged to the upper classes: charitable bequests and the establishment of schools if they were practical business men of the middle classes. The wording and contents of wills clearly reflect this change in attitude. For instance, the will of Richard Palmer of Moreton-in-the-Marsh dated 1497 ran as follows:–

> I give my body to be buried in the nave of the parish church of St. Peter, Blockley near Morton Henmarsh. To the mother church of Worcester 2/-. To the fraternity of St. John the Baptist 2/-. To the high altar of Blockley 6/8. To the parish church of Batsford 6/8. Also for a missal to be bought for the church of Bourton 6/8.

and that of John Firethorne dated 1494, as well as a bequest for a chantry at the altar of Blockley church, also mentioned:–

> To my wife, the tenement in Moreton on condition she hire a suitable priest to celebrate for my soul; and if she will not do so, the said tenement shall be sold.

In complete contrast, William Tracy of Toddington, who died in 1530, wrote in his will that he did not rely upon the works of men or upon saints or masses, but trusted to be saved only by the merits of Christ. Later this was to become the common form of Protestant wills, but at the time (i.e. before Henry VIII's breach with Rome or Edward VI's total commitment to reformed doctrine) it was deemed heretical, and the Chancellor of the diocese was ordered to exhume Tracy's corpse from consecrated ground and rebury it elsewhere. He went one step further and had the body burned at the stake, thus making Tracy, though already dead, the first Gloucestershire 'martyr' for the reformed faith.

4
The Land

'This is the new gyse . . .'

The years that saw the dissolution of the monasteries, the introduction of an English Bible and Prayer Book, and the supersession of Papal authority in England by that of the king, constituted a traumatic experience for most of those who lived through them. Without this enforced departure from traditional practices and outlook, people would not so soon have been free to act and think independently of the Church's guidance and dictation, nor been enabled to achieve, both individually and as a nation, the artistic, literary and political heights that made the late 16th century a 'Golden Age' in English history. Nevertheless, the events of the 1530's and 1540's were disturbing, and predisposed people to take an anxious attitude to other happenings. After all, if the omniscient and omnipotent Church was shown to be vulnerable and at fault, what *was* dependable?

That Gloucestershire people gradually adjusted to, rather than actively opposed religious changes, was partly explained, as we have seen, by a long established tradition of anti-clerical and anti-papal views held by members of all classes from the gentry down to the poor; it was also explained by the stable and profitable state of agriculture in the county, on which almost everyone – directly or indirectly – depended for their livelihood. Any uneasiness over religion would have been heightened by a shortage of food or other basic supplies: while against a background of serious economic distress, religious changes would have seemed inopportune if not positively dangerous.

By the 16th century the pattern of farming in Gloucestershire was firmly fixed. Necessarily, what was done and how it was done varied according to local circumstances, but a subsistence level was possible everywhere, and in the Vale and on the Cotswolds, the potentialities of the land proved to be capable of considerable expansion to meet the changes and challenges of the period. Saxton's map* of 1579, though chiefly concerned with marking geographical features and churches, at the same time reflects the minor significance of the towns in the landscape and the great number of scattered small villages and hamlets; for although by this time the county had some growing urban communities – Bristol, Gloucester, Tewkesbury,

* See page 2.

54

Stanton, a typical Cotswold village.

Cirencester for instance – and flourishing country markets, these occupied strictly limited areas and by modern standards were still small; the most numerous and characteristic settlements were in fact nucleated villages surrounded by open arable fields, pasture and commons. Some, but by no means all, had manor houses each with its own demesne, enclosed gardens and parkland.

In the Forest of Dean throughout the century the woodland remained a royal preserve, and even when granted away as happened at times (e.g. the manor of Lydney was sold in 1560 to Sir William Wynter, Queen Elizabeth's Vice-Admiral) it was for the sake of the timber and underlying coal and iron, not for clearance and cultivation, so settlements in the area continued to be small, and the growing of food-crops and keeping of livestock secondary in importance to wood-cutting, charcoal-burning, iron-smelting and coal-digging; yet without this means of supplying their own basic needs, the foresters would have been badly off and dependent on markets outside the area at Gloucester or Tewkesbury for example. The climate and soil along the valley of the Severn favoured mixed farming, and already by the 16th century in many places this had moved away from subsistence to market-based production. Barley and wheat were the chief food crops; cattle, oxen and pigs, the livestock; fruit and hops were grown mainly for cider- and perry-making and brewing; vetches, peas and oats as

The Brass of a Miner in Newland Church

Charcoal Burning

fodder; teazles, saffron, woad and weld as industrial crops to satisfy the needs of the cloth merchants. On the Cotswolds, arable farming for wheat and barley was done in conjunction with the keeping of sheep, and here too in the north and south of the region, teazles and dye crops were produced.

As a guide to the way in which the land was worked manorial records are invaluable, for here regularly each month were recorded the minutiae of the farming calendar: of the movements of men and livestock: of services fulfilled, of rents and dues outstanding: of resolutions made by common consent of all the suitors to the court for the better and more harmonious management of affairs in the coming weeks. In some ways and in some places the basic system of farming in Gloucestershire remained mediaeval, i.e. based on a system of open arable fields, where villagers had holdings of scattered strips (each usually commensurate with a day's ploughing) separated by unploughed balks:

> 'It is ordered that every tennante shall leave a furrowe of every acre and halfe acre betwene neighboure and neighboure in all the feildes . . . and that all the tennantes shall come together to do the same between Christmas and Candilmas.'

According to Marshall's* survey of agriculture in the county:

> The ancient course of the common fields was singular. Each township was divided into two fields for crop and fallow alternately – one year wheat and barley, and the next a whole year's fallow. . . .

but this was how things had begun, and by the 16th century variations on the original theme had been introduced – the arable field sub-divided to allow for autumn and spring ploughing, the fallow planted with legumes, and from time to time assarts cleared and planted with oats. However, the choice of which crops should be grown was still communally decided and adhered to:

> We . . . do hereby consent and agree with each other that the Common field where, according to the usual course of husbandry would the ensuing years be Fallow, shall be sown with such Corns or Grains as shall by each occupier of lands therein be thought proper. (Leonard Stanley)

Where there was meadowland, this too was shared, and individual strips marked with merestones. Holdings in the open fields carried entitlement to the use of common land, a highly valued right, since here animals and geese could be grazed, wood collected for fencing and repairs, and furze and turf cut for fuel. The possessive attitude of villagers in relation to the commons is reflected in their fierce opposition to the threatened loss of them by

---

* Marshall: *The Rural Economy of Gloucestershire.*

Harvesting in the Open Fields.

enclosure, and the promptness with which squatters were dealt with. Although in some parts of the county it was claimed that 'If any man in one night could erect a hut on the common and light a fire there so that smoke was seen to come up through the roof at sunrise, that man thereby earned a right of establishment'; nevertheless, more usually it was insisted on that every cottager should have four acres of land around his house (not easily engrossed out of the common) and entries in the manor records more often ran along these lines:

> Thomas Rogers has enclosed a garden on the common . . . and is ordered to open up his garden and keep it so.
> All the tenants owning common pasture at Waterton are immediately to tear up the cottage newly built there and put the old woman living there into the house of John Horewood (Bisley).

Sheep and cattle were turned on to the stubble after harvest, and then fed on hay cut from the meadow or any edible greenstuff that could be spared; and because supplies of fodder were rarely adequate, the number of animals allowed on the common land was strictly stinted. 'John West fined for overburdening the common with 20 sheep'. Officials such as a shepherd, a swineherd and a cowherd were appointed when there were large flocks to be tended, so there was no excuse for animals to wander. Any found unaccompanied were impounded and only released on payment of a fine . . . at least usually:

> The catell of 2 towneshippes were ympounded for trespassing in the grasse of the tennantes of this Lordshippe and the pounde was afterward broken in the night and all the cattell let forthe but by whome they knowe not, nor who were owners of all the said cattell (Maugersbury).

Hedges and ditches were maintained by communal effort and anyone who did not do his share of work would be fined:

> It is ordered by a comon concent that all the gappes betweene Odington hedge and the Edenbrooke to be substantially made and kepte all the yere upon payne of every man therein offending to lose 3/4. A trench in the bottom of the Slade shall be scoured before the 1st day of September, upon payment of 5/- by everyone who hath ground adjoining that shall refuse to do his purpose towards it. (Maugersbury).

Various places at different times and according to special circumstances might find it necessary to take other precautionary measures. For instance, at Bibury the villagers were expected to provide a net for catching crows 'these birds being so destructive to the grain and to all thatched structures, everyone is required to do all they can to destroy them.' Residents who neglected to keep their houses and barns in good repair were taken to task, as were parents who failed to control their children: 'Tenants presented and fined 3d a piece for suffering their children to break hedges.' The diversion of streams or the obstruction of paths that might hinder the movement of animals, carts or ploughs was punished, as was any anti-social act:

> We present a dunghill lying in the common street at Giles Freeman's stable door being a common nuisance, and if the same is not carried away by Giles Freeman within 3 weeks, and if any is laid there any more, he is to forfeit 10 sh. (Longborough).

Where manorial lords had not yet consolidated their holdings, they too had strips of land scattered throughout the arable fields and shared the use of meadow land and commons. They were also bound, as were their tenants, by commonly determined usages: 'The lord himself presented among other

tenants for breaking the stubble with sheep before the day appointed.'
Though no longer holding their dependents in personal bondage, they still
clung to certain of their seigneurial rights: the collection of heriots* on the
death of tenants: the inclusion of produce in the rents: the jealous hold over
woodland – difficult to maintain in the face of systematic stealing of trees to
make hedges, or lopping of boughs for building wood after the bark had
been stripped off for fodder: the obligation of tenants 'to grind their corn
and malt at the Lord's mill . . . and not elsewhere' and 'none shall deliver
their grist to any foreign miller to be ground from the Lord's mill.'

Who were these land-users who constituted such a large proportion of the
population of Gloucestershire? At the top end of the scale were the gentry,
some of very considerable – almost aristocratic – status, others no more
than successful yeomen newly risen to an enhanced social position; but the
situation here was rather unusual in that, except for the Berkeleys, there
were no real magnates among the landowners. In their time, the
aggressively ambitious families of the Middle Ages – the Clares,
Despencers, Mortimers and Beauchamps – had acquired a territorial
foothold in the county but had never successfully dominated its affairs; they
had now disappeared. Other old established but less aspiring families had
survived, partly because they had few political commitments, but also by
reason of a careful use and husbanding of their resources and a skilful
avoidance of responsibilities that might detract from family interests (for
example, the refusal of a knighthood in spite of a man's having the
necessary means and qualifications to support the status): and by judicious
marriages that had consolidated scattered holdings of land into compact
estates, e.g. the Hungerfords of Down Ampney with the Husseys of
Sapperton: the Casseys of Wightfield with the Fettiplaces of Swynford: the
Guises of Woodchester with the Cliffords of Frampton. The wording of
this last settlement (made in 1518) indicates the determination that, come
what may, a union of the two families should be accomplished:

> Anselm, son and heir of John Guise Esq shall marry Alys daughter of
> James Clifford Esq or another daughter of James Clifford within 10
> years of Anselm's age if Alys dies before marriage; Alys shall marry
> Anselm or another son and heir on the same terms. If both die, the
> same to apply. The costs of finding the said Anselm to his scole and
> lerning as well yn apparrell as mete and drynke tyll he accomplysh the
> age of 17 years, and also of the marriage, shall be borne equally by John
> Guise and James Clifford.

To these old families were now being added newcomers to the gentry
class, all of them in one way or another having successfully taken advantage

---

* Heriot: the due exacted by a landlord on the death of a tenant, usually the man's best beast.

Sir Thomas Leigh, Lord Mayor of London who became a Gloucester-shire landowner.

of the times. There were, for instance, yeomen and merchants who had 'thriven so well' as to be able to acquire estates and local importance: the Poynters and Cosyns of Cirencester who became landowners at Bagendon and Elkstone: the Blomers who bought land at Hatherop and within a generation had extended their estate to Eastleach Turville: and of course, best known of them all, the Tames, who started as graziers at Stowell, became wool merchants and cloth dealers at Cirencester, and finally acquired the manors at Rendcomb and at Fairford where they settled. During their lives John and Edmund Tame enriched the churches of these two places with their munificence, and after death the terms of their wills provided evidence of their worldly success – John's household comprising a large number of servants and '4 head shepherds', and Edmund's estate including 'corn, cattle and 500 sheepe in the wool.'

Then there were those who, espousing the cause of religious reform at the right moment, benefited from the re-distribution of monastic lands. Richard Tracy, although his father's keenness for reform had proved premature, went along with Henry VIII's policy, was recognised by Bishop Latimer as being 'given to good hospitality and always ready to serve the King on commissions and in other ways,' and thus gained for his family, lands from the estates of Winchcombe, Hailes and Tewkesbury to add to what they already had at Toddington. Sir Thomas Leigh, who as Lord Mayor of London at the time of Queen Elizabeth's accession, rallied Protestant support in the city on her behalf, obtained Evesham lands at Adlestrop, Longborough and Maugersbury: and Thomas Dutton, who had acted as a surveyor of monastic lands for Henry VIII and must therefore have had some knowledge of the value of them, acquired the valuable monastic grange at Sherborne and made this the nucleus of a family estate that was ultimately to stretch as far as Cheltenham. Richard Pate also, who became Recorder of Gloucester and Cheltenham's benefactor, purchased properties in these two places and at Minsterworth, after surveying the possessions of religious houses there.

Finally, thanks to the policy of the Tudor sovereigns of bringing able men – of whatever background – into their service, and of rewarding loyalty where they found it, some new families joined the ranks of the landowners in Gloucestershire. The Wynters, originally seafarers from Bristol, who had given faithful service in the Navy under Henry VIII and Elizabeth, were granted land in the Forest of Dean; John Chamberlayne was rewarded for diplomatic services abroad under Henry VII, Henry VIII and Edward VI with lands near Stow on the Wold; Nicholas Overbury, a royal judge, became lord of the manor of Bourton on the Hill; Richard Master, physician to Elizabeth I, was granted the site of Cirencester Abbey; Baptist Hicks of Chipping Campden and William Courteen of Lower Swell were helped towards these Gloucestershire estates by being ready lenders of money to the Crown.

Below the ranks of the gentry, in rural society, were the yeomen and husbandmen, 'an estate of people living in the temperate zone betwixt greatness and want', those at the top of their class scarcely distinguishable from the lesser gentry, those at the bottom – through fluctuating fortunes or generally restricted means – only narrowly able to maintain their independent status, though always anxious to prove and exploit it. The terms yeomen and husbandmen were not necessarily definitive or exclusive in themselves, since there were owners and tenants, employers of labour and farmers working single-handed, in both classes. On the whole though, the yeomen had ampler means and greater security than the husbandmen, and therefore ranked as more substantial persons socially. In villages where there was no manorial lord to dominate (and these were quite numerous in Gloucestershire) yeomen and husbandmen might form the bulk of the population, and between them own and control most of the land. Here and there, and from time to time, a family might run into misfortune and have to dispose of assets, but there was a marked social and economic stability in most places, with the same names appearing through several generations, in possession of holdings and rights, any changes in fortune being for the better rather than for the worse.

Cirencester Abbey, acquired by Richard Master physician to Queen Elizabeth I.

Whereas the gentry were in a position and ready to take advantage of opportunities to make block additions to their properties, members of the class below them tended to increase their holdings by as little as an acre at a time, trading on a neighbour's willingness or need to part with land or make an advantageous exchange. Again, while their superiors preferred to *buy* rather than to rent land for their own use, yeomen and husbandmen tended to *lease* more land to provide extra pasture or extend their arable holdings. And as the 16th century progressed, and owners of large estates improved their fortunes by careful management, investment and experiment, lesser holdings were made to yield improved returns through the hard work and individual effort of those who worked them. These people of the 'middling sort' in rural society were well-housed, fed and clothed: many were educated and some had travelled. They were proud of their independence, jealous of their rights, and because their farming activities were conducted on a considerable scale, they had money as well as the means of subsistence available, and the things that money could buy within their reach. In many cases the yeomen deliberately fixed their ambitions below their means, and while seeking a materially better living standard for themselves and their family, they avoided spending money on ostentatious social or public undertakings designed to impress their equals. Expenditure was regarded as an investment in fact, and when money could not be gainfully employed, it was saved. 'The yeomen wears russet clothes but makes golden payment, having tin in his buttons and silver in his pocket'.

The lower ranks of rural society were composed of the cottagers and the poor. Because their tenures were not as secure as those of the freeholders, in that they might have to be renewed quite frequently and on less advantageous terms each time, cottagers could be reduced to homelessness and penury, but generally they took steps to avoid becoming completely dependent on the returns of their holdings in the village fields by acquiring additional means of subsistence. They might, for instance, lease part or all of their land, thus freeing themselves to work as rural craftsmen or as hired labourers on someone else's land, and having a rent as well as wages to live on. In all villages the presence of a blacksmith, a hurdlemaker or a wheelwright was an asset, as were men prepared to undertake work in the fields; while the owners of large houses and estates were always thankful to have a pool of labour, male or female, whence to draw gardeners (women were often employed as such) stablemen, kitchen helpers and the like. Estates records show that tenants, still with enough time to work small-holdings, were also regularly employed at the big house, where as well as their wages they would be given meals while at work, afforded help for themselves and their families in times of sickness, need or old age, and offered openings in the household for their children.

In Gloucestershire though, a more lucrative additional means of

Blacksmiths

The Cottage Housewife

Haymaking

Country Pursuits.

subsistence was industrial work, i.e. the spinning and weaving of wool for the clothiers in the larger towns, who, without having to provide quarters or capital equipment for their employees, distributed raw material for them to work on in their own homes. Here the whole family would join in during the winter months when there was little to be done outside, and the women and children continue during the summer, should the men be needed, or choose, to work out in the fields. Up to twenty miles distance from the clothing towns (e.g. Cirencester, Painswick, Uley, Minchinhampton) cottagers were thus employed, the clothiers finding it well worth-while to travel so far to distribute the wool and later to collect the finished work. Although, as we shall see, the ill-effects of fluctuations in the cloth trade were handed on immediately from the merchants to their dependent employees, nevertheless for much of the century this additional or alternative means of subsistence maintained the cottagers' standard of living at a reasonable level and enabled them to acquire benefits – domestic equipment, better clothes, a more varied diet – which otherwise they could not have had. Evidence of the extent of this practice is to be found widely in manorial records, in such references as 'a parcel of land with two Rackplaces' and 'Will Esler has cut an oak on his tenement and made thereof a boome for a loome.'

The really destitute were not markedly numerous in Gloucestershire during the 16th century, but they did increase in number, and their presence is acknowledged by reports of squatters, by the appointment of 'Beadles of Beggars' to keep vagrant strangers away from the doors of local inhabitants, and of course, by the introduction of a poor rate to subsidise the unfortunates legitimately belonging to particular parishes. While the cottagers had holdings which, whether worked by themselves or leased, were sufficient to support themselves and their families, the poor had little or no land, and so were completely dependent on being employed by others for a living. Though their services were undoubtedly useful at times, if they were ill-equipped for anything but labouring they tended to be the last taken on and the first dismissed; and with few tenurial rights, the most likely to lose their homes and small plots should there be any re-arrangement of land in the village. Some of the poor were undoubtedly the victims of contemporary circumstances (e.g. inflation, enclosure projects) but some had been brought down to this level by improvidence and lack of enterprise, and accepted it as a permanent lot.

In all spheres the 16th century was a period of opportunity for those with ambition and initiative, landowners and land-users no less than others. By the end of the previous century the population of the country as a whole had recovered from the effects of the Black Death, and subsequently it was to increase steadily until by the end of the 16th century it had increased to almost half as much again. (A rough estimate is from 2.36 million to 3.80 million, a rise of 40%). The most marked effects of this rise were in the towns, and nowhere more than in London (approximately 50,000 in 1500 and 250,000 in 1600) which was steadily spilling over beyond the walls of the old mediaeval city and its westward extension at Westminster, into the surrounding countryside, drawing into its orbit outlying villages that had once been isolated settlements in a rural setting. More people created a demand for more food and goods made from agricultural products – leather, flax, wool, animal fats and malting barley – and in particular, townsfolk no longer producers of such things themselves, were dependent on obtaining them from elsewhere. So, in the vicinity of towns and especially of London, there was an expanding market for the agriculturalist to exploit if he wished, and a great number did so.

Hampton the Seat of Phillip Sheppard Esq.

Minchinhampton, a growing centre of cloth-making in the 16th century.

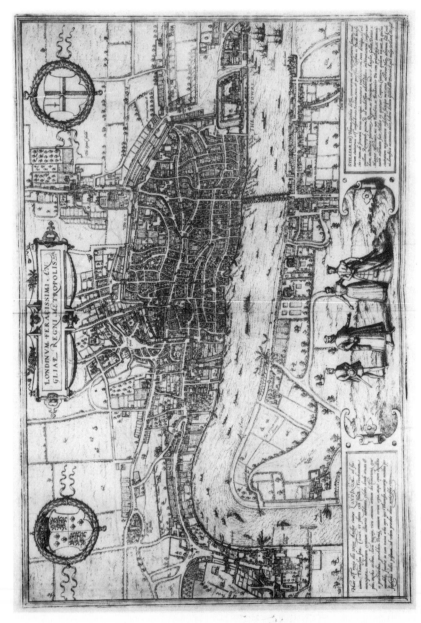

London in the 16th Century.

The existence of established communications and the expansion of trade in wool and cloth had already encouraged the rise of market centres in Gloucestershire, and to these had been added by the 16th century the flourishing ports of Bristol, Gloucester and Tewkesbury, so within the county there was a steady demand for food crops and the raw materials of industry. Gloucestershire also supplied some of the needs of the Midlands and the Welsh border counties, but even more important during the 16th century was the development of a lucrative connection with the London market, especially in cereals, meat, bacon and cheese, largely using river transport via Lechlade. So now as never before, there was an urgent need to break away from the mediaeval system of farming, which at best was only designed to produce a subsistence, and in bad times fell far short of this. Some landowners, as we have seen, had already made tentative advances towards better management of their holdings, and the promise of profit induced many more to follow suit, experimenting with new methods designed to improve production, extend the variety of crops and enable more livestock to be kept. But to achieve these ends the land had to be used more economically, and its fertility maintained. As the century progressed and the demand for wool became less pressing than the demand for food, farmers automatically tended to break up some of their pasture for arable land: to abandon the practice of leaving part of their fields fallow and unproductive for a whole year: and to find ways of increasing the yield of crops.

However, while land was still being shared by villagers and manorial lords alike, and worked according to communally agreed practices, experimental departures from the traditional regime were virtually impossible, and it was clearly essential that men should be enabled to hold their land in severalty and enclose it, if progress was to be made. Already though, by the 16th century, the idea of enclosure had emotive associations, because popular experience of the procedure to date had been unfavourable. Manorial lords had in fact begun to enclose parts of their demesne quite early on, but it was to counteract the effects of the shortage of labour consequent upon the Black Death, and simultaneously to exploit the expanding market for wool, that the practice had been adopted more generally. 'Who will be at the cost to keepe a dozen in his house to milk kine, make cheese, carry it to the market, where one poor soul may by keeping sheep get him a greater profit?' Had the new enclosures only been of existing pastures and intended for the protection of flocks there could have been few objections to them; but the profitability of keeping sheep induced many landowners to convert arable to pasture and even to engross commons and land with villagers' homes on it, at which point popular fury was aroused, and enclosing (rightly or wrongly) became synonymous with the loss of rights in the commons, shortages of food, evictions and depopulation.

On the whole the amount of feeling generated was disproportionate to the cause of it, since the making of enclosures was largely confined to areas where the soil was equally well adapted to arable or pasture (i.e. the Midlands): evictions were only feasible where tenants were few and vulnerable: and in any case the movement slowed up as the supply of wool began to level with the demand. Certainly, by the time that Sir Thomas More made his impassioned attack on enclosures in the early 16th century, there were fewer grounds for it than there had been half a century earlier; but the associations remained. So, when in due course the demand for, and prices of food supplies began to rise and there was an inducement to enclose more land – this time for the protection of crops and the pursuit of improvements – the immediate reaction was hostile, only now people were more literate than in the 14th and 15th centuries, and there were means of communication available. In pamphlets, popular ballads and plays, enclosers became familiar figures, identified as 'greedy gulls' and 'insatiable cormorants' and accused of having 'sold the righteous for silver and the poor for a pair of shoes'. They were in fact the villains of the piece for whom there was nothing good to be said – at least on the part of non-enclosers.

> The towers go down, the land decayes;
> Of cornfeldes, playne layes (meadows)
> Great men maketh nowadayes.
> A sheepecotte in the church,
> Commons to close and kepe;
> Poor folk for bred to cry and wepe.
> Towns pulled down to pasture sheepe,
> This is the new gyse.*

But by the late 16th century, although the familiar arguments were still put forward, this happened less often and with decreasing conviction. Freed by the Reformation from the restrictions placed on profiteering by the mediaeval church, many landowners were as keen to make a success of their particular enterprises as contemporary business men who were investing in overseas ventures; moreover, in their new found independence of mind and self-confidence, they were ready to prove the 'rightness' of their ideas. So against the arguments of the anti-enclosers were now arrayed the convincing results obtained by the improvers; to which, if further weight were needed, could be added the views of various writers who were beginning to publish works of comment and advice on farming (e.g. Fitzherbert, Tusser, Googe and Plat) all of whom advocated the type of experiment that forward-looking farmers had embarked on – manuring, liming and marling: the making of water-meadows to ensure a fresh bite for the sheep and lambs after a winter on short rations: the introduction of new

* From the ballad *Now-a-dayes*.

crops, especially turnips as winter feed for livestock; and mixed rather than specialised farming – 'He that hath both sheepe, swine and hive / Sleep he, wake he, he may thrive' (Fitzherbert).

Yet another argument used to justify enclosures was the fact that these were no longer being made by powerful landowners and forced on lesser folk from above, but much more often were the idea of smallholders intent on adding to their lands by consolidation and on asserting their right to do what they liked with their own property. Increasingly common in the late 16th century were agreements between villagers to exchange strips of land with each other so that individual holdings should be compact and thus more easily and economically worked.

> Upon sundry good considerations – moved between all the freeholders and customary tenants . . . and all others having landes within the circuite of the saide manor . . . it is ordayned by comen consent of the said court that sundry and divers grounds . . . shall be severed and enclosed and so kept severall . . . which enclosures cannot aptly or conveniently be broughte to pass without such exchanges being made between the said parties that thereby every of them mighte have his porcion leyed together . . . (Dowdeswell).

There were also agreements between manorial lords and villagers, the former conceding demesne or other land in order that he shall have a compact block to enclose: the latter agreeing to exchange their holdings for what the lord is granting.

> The humble petition and desire of Your Lordships tenants within the mannor of Sutton – Shewinge that the petitioners do well to observe from other places and parts of this kingdom the different advantage that is made to the Tenants and owners of lands by the enclosure and holding thereto in severalty, and finding noe Impediment in their doing thereof soe they may receive your Lordship's Approbation and Encouragement therein . . .

To which petition William, Lord Petre was pleased to consent. It would be naive to believe that in fact every single soul in a village was in full agreement with arrangements such as these. Some agreed in principle and then demurred at what they saw being put into practice; others may not have even grasped what was being mooted. All the same, there was usually an impressive list of names attached to such contracts, the wording of which leaves no doubt as to the beliefs and earnest hopes of their proposers.

In the face of this desire on the part of smallholders (as opposed to greater landowners) for the holding of land in severalty and making of enclosures, it was difficult to sustain the old traditional and emotional arguments against them, although until the end of the century there were some who continued to make the issue a test of social attitudes (i.e. individual gain

A Cotswold barn.

versus the misery of all the people). Even the central government was drawn into the conflict because, on occasions, enclosures were included among the grievances of people involved in rebellions, and official policy could not afford to ignore any potential cause of public disorder, or threat to the existing social structure on which was based the system of taxation, administration and national defence. Statutes were passed therefore (in 1489, 1515, 1536 and 1556) to preserve tillage and prevent depopulation, but from the start their enforcement was limited to certain localities and hedged in by provisos: indeed, commissioners empowered with their execution were advised to 'use theyr discretions in temporing and qualifeing . . . In some places of this Realm, yt ys not necessary the purview of this Estatute extende and bee fully executed'. As Beresford comments: 'A general prohibition was a prelude to private exemptions'; and certainly the statutes seem to have made little general impact.*

The fact that the country became more orderly as the century progressed, allowing a more relaxed attitude to prevail generally: and the wider acceptance of the belief that 'men are not to be compelled by penalty, but allured by profit, to any good exercise', gradually swung both official and public opinion round to taking a more favourable view of enclosures, and by the close of the century an attempt had already been made to get a bill passed by Parliament 'that a Man maie inclose so much Lands as himself listeth, soe it be for the maintenance of his house.' Although at this point the Commons rejected the proposal, it was in fact the first of a series of measures that during the next two centuries were to legalise single private enclosures and then general ones, until in the end not just the arable fields,

---

* Beresford: *Habitation versus Improvement.*

Quarry at Ablington.

but meadows and commons as well had become private instead of communal property. So by the end of the 16th century in Gloucestershire, the landscape was taking on a more modern look in places where the huge open fields of the community had been divided between the villagers and individual holdings hedged or fenced in: where instead of a single expanse of wheat or barley might be seen a chequered pattern of different crops and grazing grounds: and where the animals were now confined to their owner's land and no longer shared the common pastures.

Increasing supplies of agricultural produce to satisfy domestic and national demands, and an expansion of traffic in grain, livestock and dairy produce with markets in London, the Midlands and elsewhere, were a direct result of improved farming methods. The consequent profitability of land-owning and usage was reflected in a higher standard of living among all but the poorest classes, and in what William Harrison (writing in 1587) called 'the great amendment of lodging' especially noticeable in Gloucestershire, where larger and more comfortable farmhouses with a separate complement of stables, barns and outhouses replaced earlier, more ramshackle structures, in which men and animals had often sheltered under the same roof. Because the necessary materials were readily available (almost every village had a quarry) and because the local stone was quite easy to work, the new buildings seemed to grow out of the landscape and become an integral part of it, all having a common architectural style – with steeply pitched roofs, lofty chimney stacks, high gables and long ranges of mullioned windows – to which individual masons might add their own distinctive features – ornamental door porches and surrounds, gable copings, finials on roofs and date stones set in gables. All buildings, even barns and pig styes, were of a high quality. In many villages the larger dwellings lined the main street as earlier village homes had done, and although there has been some rebuilding since the 16th century, this pattern of settlement can still be seen especially in the Cotswolds where places such as the Barringtons, Naunton, Chedworth, the Duntisbournes and Broadwell have a succession of farms with imposing barns and other outbuildings.

The cottages of the poor were not so often refurbished, and because of their poor construction most of them have long since vanished; but in some places, where the clothiers had a vested interest in keeping spinners and weavers at work, they were responsible for erecting stone-built dwellings for the latter, just as some landowners were ready to ensure that their labouring tenants were better housed. This explains the existence of quite small, stone-built village homes alongside the larger farms, and the continuation throughout the century of the mediaeval pattern of the nucleated village.

While yeomen and husbandmen were acquiring improved living and working quarters, so above them, those who were moving into, or already belonged to, the ranks of the gentry, were enhancing their public image with more comfortable and dignified dwellings. Indeed, among the gentry, building, rebuilding and improvement became almost a way of life during the later part of the 16th century. Earlier, they had been too busy adding to their lands and working out ways to exploit them, but now they were in a position to provide themselves with a setting worthy of their success and social standing. Old families, who already had established homes, tended to continue to live in them, but satisfied the contemporary urge to keep up to date, by perhaps adding a new facade to the building: introducing more light through larger mullioned windows: more warmth by means of new fireplaces and chimneys, and additional rooms for family comfort and domestic convenience, reached by impressive staircases and panelled corridors. Occasionally some mediaeval features were retained such as the moats at Poulton Court and Hasfield Court and the timber framing of Chaceley Hall, but mostly these houses in keeping with the peaceful atmosphere of the 16th century were without visible means of defence and built in the characteristic local style. The Hungerfords at Somerford Keynes, the Tracys at Stanway, the Slaughters at Upper Slaughter and the Casseys at Wightfield were among those who elaborated and embellished their houses during the latter part of the 16th century.

The Porch of Ablington Manor, built for John Coxwell.

Chavenage: porch decoration with the initials ES and date 1576.

Newcomers to Gloucestershire and in some cases new members of the gentry class tended to embark on new buildings, incorporating the latest Renaissance features such as they had seen elsewhere or learned about from the books on architecture that were beginning to circulate at this time. Ablington Manor at Bibury built for John Coxwell had an imposing gabled front and a decorated porch. At Bourton on the Hill the Overbury family had panelled rooms and an impressive approach to their house under an arched gateway. Two successful lawyers, Sir Robert Atkynson, Recorder of Oxford, and Richard Pate, Recorder of Gloucester, built mansions at Stowell Park and Matson respectively. As a result of the dissolution, the site of the manor at Chavenage came into the possession of the Stephens family (formerly of Eastington) who proceeded to build a typical Elizabethan house there, rich in contemporary ornament; while the Brydges family who were granted Sudeley Castle after the downfall of Thomas Seymour,* reconstructed the Outer Court with ground floor lodgings, and a long gallery and guest suites above – perhaps in anticipation of the visits that Queen Elizabeth was to make there later.

Thus on a basis of sound use of land, from the smallholdings of villagers to the estates of the greater gentry, a prosperous and expanding farming industry was being built up in Gloucestershire during the 16th century. That prices and profits should fluctuate from time to time was inevitable, as was also the fact that national problems should repercuss into Gloucestershire, since through trade the county was now playing a part in the national economy; but the general healthiness of the situation was undoubted, also the forward–looking attitude of the land users who in some respects were anticipating developments that did not take place elsewhere until later. Proof of the enormous agricultural resources that were laid up in the great barns, stables and farmyards of the county came to light under the unhappy circumstances of the Civil Wars of the 17th century, when Royalist and Parliamentarian commanders as well as wanting to control important strategic centres such as Bristol, Gloucester and Cirencester, also realised the value of being able to use the countryside as a larder and general store for their troops. That they could requisition as many horses as they did, showed that farmers both on the Cotswolds and in the Vale were already using these instead of oxen for ploughing and transport; and that week after week landowners were subjected to and actually met demands for grain, meat, dairy produce, leather and wool indicated just how considerable were the supplies they had in hand.

---

* Seymour had started improvements at Sudeley during his brief sojourn there in 1548 with his new wife Katherine Parr who died and was buried there.

5
The Towns

'A place of considerable trade . . .'

As has already been shown, thanks to the variety of local products and excellent links with a wider hinterland, Gloucestershire was self-sufficient in basic necessities, and had a well-established network of markets and pattern of trade by the end of the 15th century. The county also had some industry and minor crafts being practised in almost every town to satisfy local needs – leather-working, tool-making, carpentry, tailoring, and brewing, for instance: and on a much larger scale, industries that supplied goods both for the home market and for export – iron from the Forest of Dean, and woollen cloth from the Cotswolds.

Although there had been trade in and out of Gloucestershire as far back as Roman times, it was undoubtedly the mediaeval traffic in wool that gave the countryside national and international significance, established the prosperity of the wool towns, and introduced an element of sophistication and inspiration into what might otherwise have remained merely parochial transactions. The arrival of foreign merchants in the area, their appearance, their manners and demands made Gloucestershire people aware of a much wider world and alerted the enterprising to the possibility of operating on a larger scale and exploiting their advantages more fully. But the growth and flowering of the wool trade in the Middle Ages was to prove merely a foreshadowing of even more successful commercial undertakings during the 16th century, due in part to natural circumstances, but much more to new and unprecedented factors that were symptomatic of the times.

One natural development was the increase in population that was almost inevitable once the country had finally recovered from the effects of the Black Death and begun to profit from the peace and increased prosperity achieved and maintained by the Tudor regime. The incidence of the Black Death had been heavy, and at a time when – even without epidemics – at least a third of the children born would have died while still young, many years were bound to elapse before the population of the country as a whole reached its former level; but thereafter more settled conditions and a steadily improving standard of living for the majority of people, pushed up numbers especially in the towns, so that places with 1,000 to 3,000 inhabitants (e.g. Cirencester, Gloucester) in the early part of the century might have doubled these totals by the end of it, and even small market

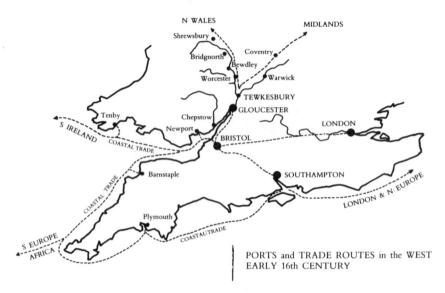

PORTS and TRADE ROUTES in the WEST
EARLY 16th CENTURY

Trade Routes of the South-West, early 16th century.

towns starting with 600 – 800 (e.g. Lechlade, Chipping Campden) might have risen to 1,000 during the same period.

Our means of estimating the number and distribution of people at any given time, or of trends in population during the 16th century, are by no means adequate, since any contemporary enumerations were made for specifically limited purposes – taxation or militia musters for instance – and inevitably missed out some categories. Parish registers of christenings, marriages and deaths introduced by Thomas Cromwell in 1538 afford a more comprehensive record but cannot help in the case of people who moved away from the place where they were born or married. The much higher number of deaths recorded in the towns for example reflects the tendency of country people to migrate thither in search of better prospects, rather than an actual local preponderance of deaths over births. However, the greater numbers – whether in the towns or countryside-created heavier demands for foodstuffs and consumer goods, and in turn stimulated farming activities and the production of raw materials for industry. In due course also, because of the rising standard of living, a market developed for

Richard Whittington, a Gloucestershire boy who made good.

more luxurious, sophisticated and unusual goods – an encouragement to merchants to step up imports from abroad.

The growth of London also might have been regarded as a natural development commensurate with that of other towns, though in the case of the capital the expansion was rapid and phenomenal: a physical encroachment along the approach roads and the banks of the Thames well beyond the confines of the mediaeval city. From the 16th century onwards until well into the 17th century, further development was discouraged and even forbidden by the government, no doubt under pressure from elements in the city who wished to retain their control of business and monopoly of profits; but the interest and determination of developers and those who were lured to the capital in search of fortunes, proved stronger than official regulations, and London went on growing. For those on the spot this was the start of social, economic and administrative problems that have lasted until the present day. For those further afield it offered a wonderful opportunity, creating an ever-expanding market for foodstuffs and the raw materials of industry. Soon all parts of the country even as far away as

Devon, Wales, the Midlands and East Anglia became part of the capital's hinterland, and Gloucestershire was to the fore in responding to this promising situation. Some goods – coal, iron, timber, cider – were despatched from ports on the Severn and thence by sea to London; animals were driven overland to the London markets for selling and slaughtering; carrier services by packhorse or wagon had already been started though these were slow and uncertain because of the state of the roads; and the bulk of goods was put on barges at Lechlade and taken the remainder of the way along the Thames – a slow but cheap and safe means of transport:

> The Lech, the Coln, the Churn and the Isis all rising in the Cotswold hills and joining together and making a full stream at Lechlade, they become one river there, also beginning there to be navigable, you see very large barges at the quay taking in goods for London which makes the town of Lechlade a very populous place.*

Among the unprecedented features of the situation in the 16th century was the vigour and enterprise that resulted from the spread of Renaissance and Reformation influences into England at the time. Seemingly the New Learning and new religious outlook not only presented unlimited fields for intellectual exploration and mastery; they also released pent up energies hitherto channelled strictly into the fulfilment of feudal and religious obligations, but now available for application to the pursuit of personal ambitions, the very idea of which had been forbidden to the conforming Christian during the Middle Ages. Not everyone was unsettled or excited by the prevailing atmosphere, nor able and inclined to take advantage of the chance to throw off old-established habits and attitudes; but enough were affected to make adventure and experiment characteristic of the period, and stories of the rise of humble men from obscure backgrounds to fortune and fame were sufficiently numerous to be readily accepted. 'Many great men were rokked in mean cradles' wrote Ben Jonson, and somewhat later but still on the same topic, Defoe commented: 'Fate has but little distinction set / Betwixt the counter and the coronet'.

A further outcome of the emancipation from traditional restrictions was a new inventiveness that was to reveal itself presently in original work of all kinds – in ship-building, aids to navigation, the weaving and dyeing of cloth; and in this sphere, success bred success, so that the tentative steps towards scientific experiment and deduction first taken in the 16th century proved the start of the scientific revolution of the 17th century. In many cases, private ambition and public aspiration were sufficient to fire enthusiasm and sustain energy; but to strengthen individual impulses and enhance

---

* Defoe: *Journeys through Great Britain.*

them with an even higher motive, there was at the time a growing spirit of nationalism, not peculiar to England, but deliberately encouraged here by the Tudors who saw in it a means, not only of harnessing men's loyalties to the sovereign and the sovereign's wishes, but also of charging various undertakings with a spiritual fervour and directing into highly profitable channels energies that might otherwise have been engaged in disturbing the internal peace of the country.

The contemporary spirit of adventure operated at all levels. In Gloucestershire the aspiring countryman betook himself to a town to seek apprenticeship, or burgess status if he could command the necessary fee and sponsorship, as is revealed in the lists of freemen in places such as Gloucester, Tewkesbury, Bristol and even London. The younger sons of the gentry, with little prospect of inheriting the family estates or benefiting from family control of church patronage, also went to towns, where – through useful contacts and/or marriage into successful merchant families – they made good, and became in time as wealthy as their elder brothers who had been saddled with the responsibility of the family homes and estates. Shrewd merchants and shopkeepers ventured into new lines of business, invested in promising ventures and risked fatal losses in pursuit of untold gains. All these had come a long way from the conservative and cautious attitude of the Middle Ages, and instead of habitually subordinating themselves to a higher authority – either temporal or spiritual – they now relied on their own judgment and conscience as the chief determinants of their actions.

And for those with the right business instincts, the opportunities were many and varied. First of all, and quite close at hand, there was trade with Ireland to be exploited. Ever since the English had begun to take an interest in exercising control over that country, whereas Chester had been the main channel of contact with Dublin and the Pale, Bristol and Gloucester had been used for trade with southern Irish ports, and the county of Gloucestershire had long been regarded as a source of conscripts, and of supplies of food and equipment for any forces that were drafted there. Although Ireland was seriously troubled with tribal quarrels, it still managed to have a thriving economy, and through its southern ports – Waterford, Cork, Kinsale and Limerick for example – passed a steady stream of goods including herring and salmon, flax and linen, many kinds of skins and leather, tallow, Irish oak (much prized for church furnishings), horses and hawks. In return for these, the Irish were anxious to import salt, iron, tools, woollen cloth and cider from Gloucestershire, as well as goods from abroad transhipped at Bristol. Throughout the 16th century trade between southern Ireland and ports on the Severn was brisk and profitable. Of this, Bristol had the lion's share: and though often regarded as undesirable because of their wild ways and unscrupulous dealings, Irishmen were listed

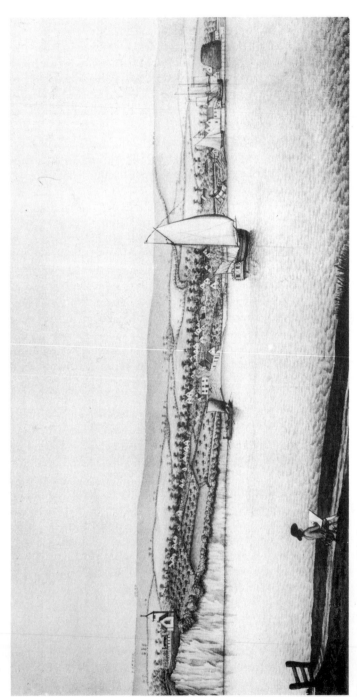

The river crossing and port at Newnham.

Thomas White, a Merchant Tailor of London with business interests in Gloucester.

among Bristol's burgesses and had their own quarter in the city – the Irish Mead. But Gloucester as well did business with Irish ports and some of the smaller ports on the Severn, such as Newnham, likewise.

> Newnham is well situated on a fine river . . . Coal is brought hither on horses' backs to be sent to other places by water. Besides the forest (of Dean) is famous for prime sorts of cider, which liquor finds a ready market here and is become a very considerable item of commerce to London and Ireland.*

Also close at hand, and potentially even more useful, there were European countries with which until the 15th century England's trading contacts had been at second hand rather than direct, since for the most part it had been foreign merchants who had been responsible for carrying English goods to Europe. Increasingly however, from the 15th century onwards, Englishmen were carrying their own wares across the Channel to the Staple port at Calais for distribution to the Low Countries, Germany,

* Defoe: *Journeys through Great Britain.*

Spain and Italy. But whereas until this point any attempt on the part of English traders to thrust their way further into the established pattern of trade in Europe would undoubtedly have aroused jealousy and active opposition, the political situation during the 16th century became so disturbed that it was unsafe and even impossible for European traders to continue using their traditional routes and markets; thus a way was opened up for Englishmen with daring and enterprise, to take over lines of business that had hitherto been foreign monopolies.

First of all the long wars in Italy (1495–1552) which also involved France, Spain and the German states, discouraged traders and craftsmen from carrying on their normal business, and in any case made the use of overland routes highly dangerous. Simultaneously, the German princes were also contending with religious strife between Catholics and the advocates of reform, i.e. the followers of Luther and Calvin, a struggle so fiercely contested as to leave most states and even the powerful Hanse towns, financially ruined. Then, from the middle of the century onwards, France was convulsed by Civil Wars that destroyed the stability and credibility of the government, rendered the whole country well-nigh bankrupt, and through death or emigration, lost it some of its most useful craftsmen. Meanwhile the Low Countries had entered into their struggle for independence from the overlordship of Spain, and cities such as Antwerp, Ghent, Bruges and Brussels having been besieged, sacked or occupied by foreign troops, lost their importance as essential focal points in the trade of Europe. As a French writer commented at the time: 'The nobles and soldiers are having a good war and the burghers are paying for everything.'

Thanks to the sympathetic rule of the Tudors, England escaped the financial ruin and the decline in morale suffered by most other states during the 16th century. In the early part of the period Henry VII's recognition of the Merchant Adventurers as well as the Staplers, and his support for English merchants in his dealings with the Low Countries and the Hanseatic League, made it quite clear that he was identifying himself with the interests of the country's trading fraternity; and during the second half of the century, the willingness of Elizabeth's Council and Parliament to take action to protect certain aspects of the economy (e.g. the woollen industry and fishing) confirmed the popular view that the Tudors were anxious to protect and even create opportunities for their subjects to make a living. Thus when English ships started to sail to Mediterranean ports to pick up the spices, dyes, silks and oriental luxuries that had hitherto been carried overland to markets in the Low Countries by Italian merchants, they felt confident of official approval; and when English companies were formed to secure trade with Russia (the Muscovy Company) and with Turkey and the Far East (the Levant Company) they easily secured official recognition and backing.

The Broad Quay at Bristol: a growing port in the 16th century.

As ports in the Low Countries and France were gradually closed because of the war situation, so London that previously had had the major share of trade with European ports lost some of the monopoly to ports in the west, particularly Bristol, that had traditional links with Gascony, the Iberian Peninsula and Italy and was now in a more favourable position than London, where in and out- going shipping had to run the gauntlet of hostile fleets in the Channel. So, during the latter half of the 16th century, it was from places along the coasts of Devon and Cornwall and the banks of the Severn, that most ships set out for Mediterranean ports with cargoes of English goods to sell, returning with raw materials, foodstuffs and luxury goods destined to be used and retailed where they were landed, or else distributed in the Gloucestershire hinterland of the Severn ports, and even further afield along the roads and waterways leading to the Welsh border counties and the Midlands. A century later, Defoe remarked that Bristol's traders had such good carrying services and so many markets in the Midlands and south-western counties that they could always count on disposing of all the goods they chose to import. This was already coming to be true in the 16th century.

However, what really swung the balance of foreign trade during the 16th century in favour of ports in the west, was the opening up of the sea routes to West Africa and the Far East, and the discovery of America, since places facing the Atlantic could command the sea routes across it. When the

John Haydon, who left a bequest to young Gloucester seafarers.

advance of Turkish power in the eastern Mediterranean (after the capture of Constantinople in 1453) closed the termini of the land routes from the Far East and thus cut off the people of Europe from their essential supplies of spices, and less essential but equally desirable silks, ivory, gold and jewels, it was the Portuguese who began to explore an alternative route to the source of these supplies down the coast of West Africa, round Cape Horn and across the Indian Ocean. For awhile they monopolised the fruits of their discoveries, but by the mid 16th century English traders out of Bristol were also visiting the Guinea Coast to pick up spices and slaves, and even venturing as far as India. Earlier, in 1497, John Cabot had set off, also from Bristol, to find a north-west passage to the Far East, and landed in Labrador, to be followed a few years later by Warde, Ashehurst and Thomas who reached Newfoundland. These were by no means isolated examples. The Spanish Ambassador noticed and commented in 1498: 'The people of Bristol have sent out every year for the last seven years, two three, or four light ships in search of the island of Brazil'. Nor was the spirit of enterprise confined to Bristol. Gloucester also must have had its seafarers, since John Haydon in his will dated 1579 left the sum of one hundred pounds to 'twoe younge men of the Citie of Gloucester, being marchaunts trading on the seas . . . to occupye for their best profitt and advantage.' At the end of four years they were expected to be in a position to repay the capital so that it could be used 'by twoe other younge men of the same citie'

But even though, in due course, the discovery of America was to have marked effects on personal fortunes and national economies (especially in so far as Mexican and Peruvian silver helped to promote and aggravate inflation) the temptation to overestimate its importance at this stage must be resisted. Until the latter part of the 16th century comparatively few people had accurate knowledge of the newly discovered lands across the Atlantic, and even those who had actually seen them tended to embellish their accounts for the sake of effect, and thus convey an impression that was anything but realistic. Primarily also, the routes explored and contacts made, meant no more than new sources of food and raw materials; only gradually did they lead to the establishment of markets to serve as outlets for English goods. Nevertheless, the voyages in themselves created a demand for more, larger and better equipped ships, stores and crews, and it was the ports on the Severn and their Gloucestershire hinterland that helped to supply these.

Inevitably, as the 16th century progressed, to satisfy the needs of an expanding and increasingly wealthy population at home and of overseas traders, the manufacture of consumer goods was stimulated. As we have seen, Gloucestershire already had its industries, mainly concerned with wool and iron, both capable of being extended and elaborated to meet current demands – woollens by means of new dyeing and finishing processes, and iron by the introduction of improved methods of smelting, particularly furnaces driven by water power. By the end of the century, finer and coloured versions of the county's plain white broadcloth were being produced in the developing clothing towns – Cirencester, Stroud and Minchinhampton for instance, and in a few places silk and linen thread and material were also appearing. Iron goods were traditionally an important factor in Gloucestershire's economy. Since the Conquest, the county had been the main source of horse-shoes and horse-nails for the king's forces, and rods of iron for making nails for the king's ships. By the 16th century tools, agricultural and military equipment were also in demand, and bells – founded at Bristol and Gloucester. Other minor and some new industries also became more important during the course of the century, the making of glass and stoneware helped by the expansion of the brewery and mineral water trade, pins, paper, pottery, leather goods, brassware, soap, and timber produced for furniture and building. In fact, Gloucestershire was already experiencing a minor industrial revolution.

In connection with this industrial expansion it is worth noting another result of the wars in Europe, namely the flood of refugees from the Low Countries and France that started to reach England in the 1560's and continued for the next 30 years or so. Mostly these were educated, middle class people, in fact the burghers who had been 'paying for everything', whose work as lawyers, bankers, merchants and craftsmen had been interrupted or even destroyed, and whose initiative and freedom of thought and conscience had been threatened by the dictatorial regime of Spain in the Netherlands or the Catholic party in France. Their arrival here was most fortuitous since they brought with them a knowledge of more sophisticated methods and in some cases completely new processes just at a time when English craftsmen were seeking to increase and improve their output to satisfy demands both at home and abroad for more refined and expensive goods.

For the most part, the Dutch refugees came into England via London and settled in the eastern and south-eastern counties, as did many of the Huguenots from France; but Gloucestershire also received its share of immigrants whose knowledge and expertise undoubtedly helped to improve the processing and finishing of woollen cloth, to extend the making of silk and linen, and to promote paper and glass-making in the county. Two famous clothing families, the Playnes and the Clutterbucks, had Huguenot origins. In Gloucester, it was reported at the end of the 16th century 'one Hoe, a Frenchman hath built a glass house and furnace, and doth make great quantities of glasses.' The Courteens, makers of, and traders in silk and linen, came from the Low Countries to London, acquired a vested interest in voyages to the East and West Indies, and ultimately established their own fleets for trading with those parts. They also acquired a reputation for privateering and smuggling but preserved their public image by a readiness to lend some of their gains – both honestly and ill-begotten – to the Crown. By the opening years of the 17th century the family had acquired a title, gentry status and were soon to become landowners at Lower Swell.

Since in due course, woollen cloth was to replace wool as the chief money- making product of Gloucestershire, it was the skills learned from the immigrants in dyeing and varying the finish of the cloth that proved most significant among 16th-century developments. In his time, Edward III had complained of the English clothiers that 'they knew no more what to do with their wool than the sheep that wears it'. Now two centuries later Gloucestershire cloth was already becoming widely known and sought after, especially the blue made at Uley and Dursley and the scarlet of Stroud. A law of 1557, forbidding the manufacture of cloth in areas outside towns, specifically excepted 'any villages near the river Stroud *where cloths have been made for twenty years past*'; and it is recorded that by the early years of the 17th century, three clothiers at Uley were selling the work of 29 local weavers. An interesting result of this industrial progress in Gloucestershire was the complete volte-face it occasioned in the popular attitude to immigrants. Even though imbued with more than a hint of opportunism, there was no doubting the willingness to welcome foreigners who had formerly been so much disliked and distrusted:

Happy the yeoman's house into which one of the Dutchmen did enter, bringing industry and wealth along with them; such as came in strangers within doors, soon went out bridegrooms and returned sons-in-law, having married the daughters of their landlords who first entertained them; and those yeomen in whose houses they harboured, soon became gentlemen and gained great estates to themselves.

The development of trade and the expansion of towns went hand in hand, for each needed and was fostered by the other. We have already noted the existence of towns in Gloucestershire from Anglo-Saxon times, and their success reflected in the establishment of weekly markets and annual fairs. Circumstances in the 16th century furthered this progress; they also determined that the towns should become more urbanised and more markedly different in character from the countryside with which, until now, they had been inextricably bound up. Although in the case of London and some provincial cities, expansion included a suburban sprawl outside mediaeval boundaries, in most places it was in-filling that supplied the necessary extra accommodation, houses being built in the rectangular plots behind street-facing premises and in the small orchards and gardens that previously had been common features of townscapes. Also, at a time when people were beginning to enjoy a greater freedom of movement than ever before and many were tending to make for the towns in search of better prospects, the freeing of ecclesiastical estates as a result of the dissolution of the monasteries and chantries, made more space available for housing larger populations. Possibly the most quoted example of the conversion of monastic property to secular use is William Stumpe's acquisition of Malmesbury Abbey for a woollen mill; but Gloucester too can provide a parallel. Sir Thomas Bell, a manufacturer of caps, purchased the site of the Black Friars, subsequently turning the church into 'a handsome mansion which was called Bell's Place', and the remaining building into a workshop employing 300 men. The area must have been considerable because even after the addition of new buildings there were still 'orchards and gardeynes adioyninge.' Bell also acquired a chantry chapel which he converted into an almshouse 'for six poor folkes.'

The greater affluence of established town dwellers was reflected in the rebuilding and enlarging of their houses and workshops, and in Gloucestershire where local stone and skilled masons abounded, a permanent pattern began to emerge, with well-built houses fronting streets that were wider and less tortuous than their mediaeval counterparts, and some permanent structures taking the place of the temporary stalls that appeared at markets and fairs, as at Chipping Campden where there was 'a middle row of new houses which appeareth very amiable and is of itself a great ornament to the town'. Cirencester begain to acquire its comfortable, settled look at this

Sir Thomas Bell: Mayor and property developer of Gloucester.

time, and of Tewkesbury it was reported 'the streets (are) long and large, decently pitched with pebbles and sweetly kept.' Tetbury had 'four streets crossing in the centre of it, consisting of abour 400 houses, chiefly built of stone and which make a handsome appearance', and Gloucester too was described as 'a fair city, not inaptly named, as its four principal streets are spacious and well-built.' Tewkesbury acquired a new Town Hall in 1586, built at a cost of £63. 17s. 7d, and one of its citizens, Thomas Poulton, devised money in his will 'towardes the erectinge and buyldinge of a Markett house in the Towne of Newent' where he had property.

Along with their surroundings, town dwellers themselves were changing in character. Increasing success in a particular craft or trade depended on greater specialisation, and gradually leading residents severed the links that had tied them to the surrounding countryside. A few remained part-time husbandmen, still holding on to and exploiting their rights in the common fields outside the town; some kept their garden plots and orchards, where they grazed a few pigs and geese and grew greenstuff and herbs for domestic use, but mostly these areas were being used for new storehouses

The 16th-century Market Hall at Tetbury.

and workshops or sold for house building. Inventories, describing the
contents of houses room by room, indicate the extent to which interior
space was being reorganised to separate working areas from the rest of the
house and to afford greater privacy and comfort to the owner and his
family. Their detailed lists of raw materials, equipment and finished goods
also reflect an intensive concentration on commercial and industrial
undertakings, which threw those who practised them into complete
dependence on others for food and raw materials necessary to life and
business, an encouragement to producers elsewhere but a situation with
built-in hazards since shortages of any kind could create acute problems that
neither local nor national administration was yet able to cope with.

   In response to the increasing and increasingly sophisticated demands of
urban populations, a wider range of services appeared. To the bakers,
butchers, brewers, carpenters, masons and saddlers who supplied basic
needs, were joined haberdashers, mercers, glovers, pewterers and
upholsterers. Gloucester, as well as its local specialists – the pin-makers,
bell-founders and glass-makers – had a goldsmith, a furrier, a hatter and an
apothecary. Winchcombe had a physician and a musician, Chipping
Campden a pargeter and a gardener, Tewkesbury a bottle-maker and a
paperman.* None of these could have made a living except in a town, but

---

* These occupational details are listed in Smith: *Men and Armour*, a schedule of men in
Gloucestershire capable of bearing arms, drawn up for the Lord Lieutenant in 1608.

THŌ. POVLTON.

THOMAS POVLTON OF TWKXBER BENEFICTER TO THE CITIE OF GLOCESTER
HE GAVE VNTO THE SAME CITIE OF GLOSESTER, CC. POWNDES FOREVER.

Thomas Poulton: a benefactor to Gloucester and Tewkesbury.

once established there, they offered goods and services useful and tempting to outsiders, as well as to local customers. Already the appearance of the town and the material comforts available there made an impressive contrast with the surrounding countryside and its accompanying standard of living. Town buildings became a model for village development: town fashions in clothes, food, pleasures, the objectives of countrymen's admiration and ambitions.

> For they of the country do ever take heed
> How they of the city do wear their weed.

The increase in urban populations and the elaboration of their needs inevitably made greater demands on local administration. More officers were called for, to deal with problems of law and order, and to enforce new regulations as they were introduced, one of the most noteworthy of these being the appointment of Beadles to deal with the number of beggars that was becoming an embarrassment and even a menace in the towns by the end of the 16th century. Tewkesbury was typical of most places in the steps taken:

It is ordered that there shall be within this borough a Beadle of the Beggars to keep from the doors of the inhabitants thereof, all vagabonds and wandering persons that shall beg alms and shall not be dwelling there.

Gloucester, being a larger town, had a more serious poverty problem than most others. Certainly, recurring items in the borough accounts were for 'cords and whips made and bought for whipping off vagabonds' and for men 'dryving the cart where the vagabonds were tyed and so brought about the citie and scourged.'

Another tendency was for town government to become more oligarchical and less democratic than it had been earlier. The social difference between the owners of the imposing houses that fronted the market square or main streets and those who lived in the smaller properties crowded behind them, was reflected in the widening gap between those who were considered eligible for civic office and those who now neither could, nor would dare to, aspire to it. In fact wealth, and not mere membership of the community was coming to be a necessary qualification for those who undertook public responsibilities, since officials had to pay fees on taking up their posts and subsequently bear the cost of special robes, lavish entertainment and innumerable incidental expenses. Moreover, if their predecessors had been improvident and left the town with unpaid debts, incoming officials might have to shoulder these burdens too, as happened at Gloucester during the 1570's. Claims in borough records: 'When Mr. Mayor was brought home: for Rosemary and bayes for a garland: for Music for our dinner: for lights to light us home': were probably all met by Mr. Mayor himself. A recognition of such obligations is seen in the will of Gregory Willsheire of Gloucester, dated 1585, wherein he left a sum of one hundred pounds to provide wine at the election of new mayors. The money for the wine was to be raised by lending five tradesmen for five years the sum of twenty pounds, 'they paying a Gallon of wine yearly' in return.

Also encouraging this emergence of an élite amongst the townsfolk was a tendency for some craftsmen to assume a superiority over others, just as merchants and lawyers believed themselves to be above artificers and shopkeepers; and while some wealthy men deliberately avoided public office because of the holes it would make in their pockets, others evidently considered that the advantages of enhanced status more than outweighed the expense this involved. The hierarchy of callings is evident in the borough records of Gloucester and Tewkesbury where high office was reserved for the socially superior. At Gloucester, John Cooke, a mercer, was four times elected Mayor; John Falkner and Sir Thomas Bell, cap-makers, three times each; and Robert Hendley, bell-founder, five times.

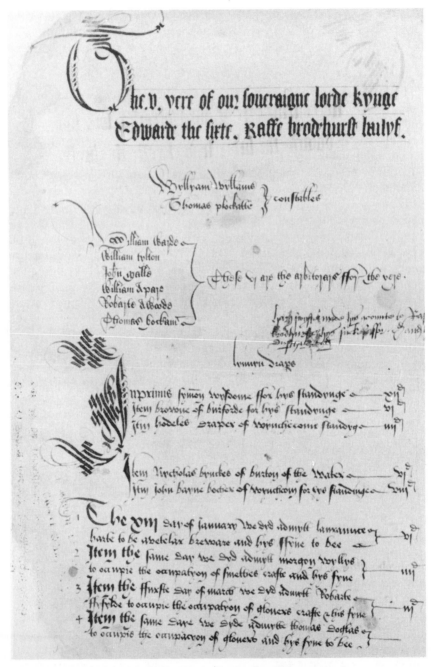

A page from the records of Northleach with details of stallage and apprentice fees.

Gregory Willsheire: made provision for Mayoral elections in Gloucester.

Evidently all these trades were well-respected, or was the success of those who practised them even more significant? Certainly the wealth that was such a help towards gaining office might well secure a person in it afterwards, and even bring dividends. The case of Thomas Rich, a mercer of Gloucester in the 17th century, no doubt had antecedents:

> [He] bought a vote for himself as Mayor by affording an alderman the office of bellman worth £20 a year. When elected he sold the city a large number of shrouds for victims of the plague; many of the shrouds were too short but all of them were expensive.

To special robes were soon added special regalia – chains of office, a civic seal, staves and a mace, and bearers to carry these – so that the mere passage of an official from one part of the town to another would involve a minor procession: attendance at church on Sundays, or at civic junketings, a major one. But whereas, before the Reformation, publicly celebrated occasions – Saints' Days and Thanksgiving – had involved all the townsfolk as participants, now the poor and less exalted were mere observers of the pomp and circumstance that surrounded those set in authority above them.

Stow on the Wold: the Grammar School founded in 1494.

It was an old claim that 'Town air maketh free'; but clearly, by the end of the 16th century, it had made some freer than others.

Although primarily still centres of trade and sources of supply for their locality, the towns were now fulfilling other functions also. To be successful here demanded certain skills and some learning as well (an ability to read and write was a condition of apprenticeship in many guilds) so the need for educational facilities was recognised quite early, and to what the church could offer in this field, the guilds and charitable benefactors added secular establishments. The abbeys of Bristol, Gloucester, Cirencester, Winchcombe and Tewkesbury all had schools attached to them, and the first three had chantry schools too; there had been a Grammar School at Wotton under Edge since 1384, at Newland since 1443, at Chipping Campden since 1487, and Stow on the Wold since 1494. As a result of the Reformation, ecclesiastical schools were closed down at the same time as the abbeys and chantries to which they were attached, but in the case of Bristol and Gloucester immediately replaced by others under the civic authorities, lest their advantages to the community be lost. At Gloucester also the Crypt School was started, on land that had belonged to Lanthony Priory, and been bought by Joan Cooke with money left by her husband, 'for a continuall free scole of Grammer for the continyall erudicion and teachingof children and Scolers ther forever.'

In other places likewise, thanks to similar benefactions, schools were started that were to ensure a useful education for future generations of townsfolk. Hugh Westwood of Northleach in 1559 left money for the founding of a school and made it incumbent on the town 'to prepare a house convenient for the schoolhouse and schoolmaster meet and necessary for that purpose – or else the school not to be there.' At Tewkesbury in 1576 a free school was begun 'by the benevolence of the inhabitants' aided by a bequest from William Ferrers. For its part, Cheltenham was indebted to Richard Pate who endowed Corpus Christi College at Oxford with property he had bought, on condition that-three quarters of the income from it should be used 'for the perpetual maintenance and foundation of a Free Grammar School at Cheltenham.' A short time later, in 1610, the will of Sir William Romney ensured not only the foundation of a school at Tetbury but also its practical use. '£13 to be paid yearly to a schoolmaster to teach the children of the parish, the schoolmaster shall be very skilful in arithmetic which art teacheth much wit.' Later, when the civic authorities took over responsibility for paying and supervising the master, they decreed that 'he shall teach the Latin tongue by the use of Lilly's Grammar . . . and in like manner for the Greek by such grammars and authors as are most usual and not by any quaint, strange or new devices of his own.'

Not only in the sphere of education did the towns assume what had previously been the role of the church; they also took over responsibility for alms-giving and the care of the sick. Usually with the help of benefactions, they began to maintain hospitals and almshouses, so that there was shelter and care available, as well as money to provide food, fuel and clothes for a number of those who would otherwise have been homeless and destitute. William Chester and Richard Shepham at Stow on the Wold, William Edgeleys and Thomas Dutton at Northleach, Richard Pate at Cheltenham, William Jones at Newland, and successive mayors of Gloucester, all subscribed to such good causes, and among the latter, John Cooke made special provision for the repair of St. Bartholomew's Hospital to keep the poor people there 'from the daunger of the great waters in the wynter time'. The authorities at Northleach were typical in appointing Governors to manage the affairs of the almspeople (nominated by the borough officials) and to examine their morals, 'expelling those absent from church and brawlers, scoulders, drunkards or any otherwise misliving people.' Other charities dispensed by the towns from money left in trust for the purpose, took the form of dowries to enable 'poor maidens' to marry, apprentice fees for young craftsmen, and interest-free loans to unfortunate tradesmen who needed help to tide them over a period of hardship.

To a majority of people though, more important than any of the foregoing, was the capacity of the towns to provide entertainment. By the 16th century life in general was less of a strain and more eventful than it had been earlier; all the same, for country folk it was still the weekly town

Chipping Campden: almshouses built by Sir Baptist Hicks.

markets and the seasonal fairs that punctuated an otherwise rather monotonous existence and exercised an irresistible attraction, with their array of
necessities and exotic luxuries for buying, and in the case of the fairs,
entertainments beyond the range of the imagination – jugglers, dancers and
performing animals. At other times too, the towns could provide diversions
unknown in the countryside, processions of dignitaries on civic occasions,
and of magistrates when courts were in session: performances financed by
the town authorities or private patrons: and even executions, which seem to
have had a macabre fascination for the onlookers. At Tewkesbury in 1599
'the church-wardens did set forth three stage plays to be played in the abbey
at Whitsuntide', while the following pleasures were listed in the Cham-
berlain's accounts at Gloucester:

> Maister Kyngeston's Abbott of Mysrule commyng to the Citie in the
> Cristmas tyme. Master Arnold's servants on May Day at the bringing
> in of May: and persons that daunced the Moorys daunse the same time.
> Lord Ambrose Dudley's players, playing openly in the Boothall.

Most outstanding of all entertainments were of course royal progresses
and royal visits. Three sovereigns honoured Gloucester in the 16th century,
Henry VII in 1486, Henry VIII in 1535 and Elizabeth in 1573, and although

these visits involved the city in enormous expense, this was outweighed by the pleasure and prestige afforded by the royal presence. We are not told what individuals spent on new clothes and entertainment, but the borough accounts record that gifts of oxen and a purse of gold were presented to Henry VIII and Anne Boleyn, and that among those rewarded were the footmen of the King and Queen, the King's trumpeters, and the servants of the King's buttery and pantry. On the occasion of Elizabeth's visit, money was paid to:

> The Queen's Majesty's bearward for bayting of this bears.
> The Queen's juggler for showing pastimes and other of his juggling feats.
> The Queen's Majesty's players: spent upon them at the tavern: for a pound of candelles at the same play: for the making of a scaffold in the Boothall.

The image of the town was indeed gloriously technicoloured to those whose lives – rather like the clothes they wore – tended to be somewhat drab.

Neverthless, desirable as the prospect of life in a town might be, for some it was merely a means to an end, this being the acquisition of a country estate and removal there to achieve finally the life of a landed gentleman. Lambard described London as a 'rich and wealthy seed plot whence Courtiers, Lawyers and Merchants be continually transferred and do become new plants among the ancient stocks', and certainly Gloucestershire was one area where new families took root during the 16th century. The Chamberlaynes, Leighs, Atkyns, Hicks and Overburys were all transplanted from London. And on a smaller scale the towns in Gloucestershire were also seed beds. The Wynters and Chesters rose to fortune in Bristol, then established themselves as landowners at Lydney and Almondsbury respectively. The Tames, whom we have already noticed, moved from farming at Stowell into trade at Cirencester, and thence to estates at Fairford and Rendcomb. Thomas Poulton of Tewkesbury and Richard Pate of Cheltenham both had, and exploited, business connections in Gloucester, but at the same time were building up considerable estates in the surrounding countryside. All these and many more proved the point made by a contemporary:

> There exists no privileged order to whom Honour and Dignity exclusively belong, but their Acquirement is Open to All who have energy to pursue them; and this observation is confirmed by daily instances of persons raising themselves from the most humble to the most elevated stations by means honourable to themselves and useful to the Community.*

* Wilson: *The State of England AD 1600.*

6

Administration

'We will be served with such men what degree soever as we shall appoint.'

In 16th century England, the mainspring of authority in government and the power that held society together, was the monarchy. The Tudor sovereigns had a capacity both to assess the needs of the country and to satisfy these, and as a result they gained the confidence and loyalty of the people, which was an all-important factor in their success. Unlike their contemporaries in Europe, the Tudors ruled without an army and without resorting to absolutism, the most favoured form of government at the time; instead they relied on popular support of and acquiescence in their policies, a trust that proved to be well-placed. Their appeal was essentially a personal one, and it was a happy chance that brought to the throne a succession of monarchs (in particular Henry VII, Henry VIII and Elizabeth) of outstanding character, vitality and magnetism, just at a time when the English were stirring themselves out of accustomed ruts and awaking to the possibilities of a wider world and a promising future.

While identifying themselves closely with the interests of their subjects and on occasion seeming to rub shoulders with them, the Tudors at the same time surrounded themselves with a certain aura that impressed their grandeur on all who came into contact with them. Both Henry VIII and Elizabeth inspired an instinctive obeisance in all but their most extreme critics, and the sight of the royal person and a gesture of royal greeting was enough to produce bows and curtseys from those in their immediate vicinity, cap-waving and cheers from those further away. 'In pompous ceremonies, a secret of government doth much consist' wrote a contemporary, and certainly the Tudors understood the importance of rigid, dignified conventions when determining the daily programme of court life, and of splendid, colourful displays of fashion and magnificence when they were making progresses between their palaces and round the country.

During their reigns, Gloucestershire was visited by Henry VII and Elizabeth of York, by Henry VIII and Anne Boleyn, and by Elizabeth I. On each occasion, though there were public receptions, entertainments and

Queen Elizabeth I, her left foot on Ditchley (Oxon) visited during a progress to Gloucestershire in 1592.

presentations in the towns along the royal route, the sovereigns were accommodated by private people, pleased or at any rate prepared, to impoverish themselves in return for the honour of having royalty under the family roof. On the occasion of his visit to Gloucester in 1486, Henry VII 'dyned at Acton with Sir Robert Poyntz, Shyref of Gloucestershire'. The Tames, rejoicing in their newly attained gentility, must have felt proud to offer hospitality to Henry VIII in their manor-house at Fairford. Sir Giles Brydges* with his wife Frances entertained Elizabeth three times at Sudeley Castle, and like many of his contemporaries, added to and improved the living quarters of his home in order to have adequate and suitable accommodation not only for the Queen but also for the host of attendants and servants who made up her household, and the several hundred carriages and waggons that transported them and their effects during the progress.

Nor was Sudeley lacking in entertainment. The looked-for music, dancing, speeches and gifts were all provided and during Elizabeth's last visit in 1592 the pageantry lasted several days and included a novelty – some Cotswold shepherds and country folk (instead of nymphs, gods and goddesses) who coupled expressions of loyalty with heavy hints about their extreme poverty, and presented the Queen with the fleece (unwashed) of a Cotswold sheep:

> These hills afford nothing but cottages and nothing can we present to your Majesty but shepherds . . . We carry our hearts at our tongues' ends being as far from dissembling as our sheep from fierceness . . . This lock of wool, Cotswold's best fruit and our poor gift, we offer to your Highness: in which nothing is to be esteemed but the whiteness, Virginity's colour: nor to be expected but duty, shepherd's religion.

No doubt this was one of the occasions when royal courtesy and graciousness were sorely tried and when, as Elizabeth remarked on another occasion: 'To be a king and wear a crown is more glorious to them that see it than it is a pleasure to them that bear it.' Neverthless, whatever the cost to the entertainers and the entertained, such occasions were invaluable in establishing the royal image vividly in the minds of the people and endowing it with an effective reality.

But the monarchs could not be everywhere at one time nor could they give their personal attention to all the details of government. They needed a means of projecting their authority to the far corners of their kingdom and of keeping a finger on the pulse of those parts, and this was to be found in their Privy Council, a body of men chosen by and entirely subject to the monarch, not necessarily uniform in outlook but completely unanimous in their readiness to devote all their abilities and resources to royal service. Because of deaths, attainders and forfeitures during the Wars of the Roses,

* Inherited the title of Lord Chandos in 1573.

Lady Frances Brydges, hostess to Queen Elizabeth at Sudeley Castle.

the aristocracy (traditional source of advice and help in government) was seriously depleted at the time of Henry VII's accession, but in any case he would have avoided employing any of his over-mighty – and therefore potentially dangerous – subjects, looking instead for co-operation and support to those ranks of society where royal favour would be valued, since it could make all the difference between mere self-satisfaction and public recognition of enhanced status and importance. This policy was continued by Henry's successors, and his son Henry VIII actually announced it in so many words: 'We will not be bound of necessity to be served with lords but with such men what degree soever as we shall appoint.'

The Privy Council therefore consisted of those who could give useful service at any particular time: consequently its personnel changed. None could claim membership as of any right save that of being summoned by the monarch; none could complain if not included. Representing every aspect of royal authority, the Council had administrative, financial and judicial functions, and could also exercise prerogative powers in so far as its decisions were sometimes given the force of law. The increasingly complicated needs of a healthy and active society during the 16th century added steadily to Council business, until from a few mornings each week its sessions were extended to the whole of every day including Sunday, some members attending only when the business in hand was their particular concern – the drafting of measures for introduction into Parliament, decisions about taxation, consideration of foreign affairs, the nomination of Justices, the questioning of informers. The main departments of administration – the Exchequer, Star Chamber, the King's Bench – were all originally offshoots of the Council, and during the 16th century three others were added – the Court of High Commission to deal with religious matters, and the Councils of the North and of Wales to deal with affairs generally, and in particular with the maintenance of law and order in these localities. Although primarily concerned with the Marcher counties along the border between Wales and England, the jurisdiction of the Council of Wales extended over Gloucestershire as well. Its President was usually the Lord Lieutenant of the county: its twenty members might include Gloucestershire Justices; some of its sessions were held at Tewkesbury and Gloucester: and many of the cases brought before it involved Gloucestershire people. Thus the county was always aware of royal authority working in its midst, and of a swift, equitable dispensation of justice emanating therefrom: 'The best cheap court in England for fees, and there is great speed made in trial of all causes.'

The Council of Wales representing the authority of the monarchy, dealt with civil and criminal cases and any disorders likely to disturb the peace of the border counties; also representing the monarch and holding a watching brief over Gloucestershire in particular was the Lord Lieutenant, an official

Sir Giles Brydges, Lord Lieutenant of Gloucestershire in the late 16th century.

introduced by the Tudors to take overall responsibility for the maintenance of law and order. Unlike most other royal appointments made from lower ranks in society, the Lord Lieutenant was nearly always a peer and a member of the Privy Council, automatically commanding respect because of his social status, and administratively useful since he was well acquainted with the locality and known to the people there. His main work was military – to ensure that the county was in a state of preparedness for any eventuality that might arise; so he was responsible for keeping a record of the men capable of bearing arms, and of the number of weapons available, and of the state of the alarm beacons on the hill tops; and in the event of any emergency – a threat of invasion, food shortages, the need for an extraordinary levy of taxes, resistance to the enforcement of some new regulation – he was expected to take the required action. The judicial records of the county were also entrusted to him. The Earl of Pembroke, the Earl of Berkeley and Sir Giles Brydges of Sudeley held the office of Lord Lieutenant in Gloucestershire during the 16th century.

In fact since the Lord Lieutenant himself had to spend much of his time in attendance at the Privy Council, his work was carried out by deputies, usually two though there might be as many as six, chosen from among the most active of the local gentry, to whom the Lord Lieutenant sent his instructions. More often than not, the latter would be prefaced with 'Forasmuch as I am not at present within your County and cannot immediately give orders upon any Emergency, I must and doe require you carefully to perform what is herein required'. . . Thus it was the deputies who actually mustered the array at regular intervals and inspected the weapons available: who reported local problems and carried out orders designed to solve them. Among others, members of the Leigh, Kingston, Dutton, Hungerford and Chamberlayne families acted as deputies. They were men who had shown a willingness to serve the community, who had usually already held the office of Sheriff, and who by education and experience were equipped to deal with practical military and administrative matters as well as more academic legal ones.

The authority of the Lord Lieutenant and his deputies was an overall one, and theirs was the ultimate responsibility for the maintenance of a satisfactory state of affairs in the county both in peaceful and precarious times. To deal with the details of day-to-day administration, there were the Justices of the Peace, an establishment instituted for keeping the peace long before the 16th century, but adapted and expanded by the Tudors to engross almost all aspects of local government. According to Tanner 'to those who were faithful over a few things, jurisdiction over many was given'; and Lambarde, whose book *Eirenarcha*, published in 1581, described in detail the work of the Justices, listed 309 statutes which in some way or another added to their duties. These men were all landowners of some standing in their locality; they had independent means derived from their estates or investments; their training had necessarily included a period at University or the Inns of Court: and they were sufficiently leisured to be available individually to deal with the mixture of judicial and administrative work imposed on them, and together to hold regular sessions to enforce the law in cases of active transgression. As well as listening to complaints, promoting enquiries into a variety of offences and making arrests, they issued licences to alehouse keepers, strolling players and legitimate beggars (disabled soldiers and sailors): supervised the maintenance of bridges and highways: and enforced regulations in respect of wages and prices. Towards the end of the century their work was enormously increased by the Recusancy Laws,* and by the elaboration of the Poor Laws, in which connection the Justices had to concern themselves not only with the punishment of rogues but also with enforcing the collection of a compulsory rate in each parish for the relief of the deserving poor.

Like the Lord Lieutenant, the Justices were closely identified with the work of the Privy Council in that they were nominated by the latter and answerable to it. Continually, they received orders from it, and Sir Thomas Smith in his *De Republica Anglorum* asserted that lest they should relax their efforts (which, to be fair, was unusual) 'every year the Council chooseth out certain articles out of penal laws already made, to repress the evil rule of the populace and sendeth them down to the Justices, willing them to look upon these points.' Being well informed about local affairs and people, and always ready to serve – unpaid, save for the expenses they were allowed to claim when attending the Quarter Sessions – the Justices were reliable and invaluable agents of Tudor policy, and proof of this lay in their being summoned to Westminster from time to time for consultation with the Privy Council. At first there were only four Justices to each county, but pressure from members of the gentry class anxious to achieve this distinction, as well as official recognition of their usefulness, led to the numbers being increased until Gloucestershire on average had about thirty.

Names that will now be familiar to readers were to be found continually among the Justices – Tame, Hungerford, Tracy, Wynter, Dutton, Guise, Leigh, Chamberlayne – and it says much for their devotion to duty that these men continued in office for years and consistently commanded respect and liking among the people they were dealing with. Clearly they exercised their authority with tact and discretion, especially when it came to enforcing Sumptuary Laws:† conducting investigations into the breaking of fences, robbing of orchards or the 'spreading abroad of false, seditious and slanderous news': keeping order at fairs and wakes: or doing the work of a health committee in times of plague. Understandably, contemporary opinion decided: 'there was never in any commonwealth devised a more wise, a more dulce and gentle, nor a more certain way to rule the people, whereby they are kept always as it were in a bridle of good order.'

Understandably also, any exception to the generality of good sense and moderation stood out. Sir Anthony Kingston, for instance, as the King's Provost Marshal, had helped to put down the Pilgrimage of Grace in 1536, and opposition to the new Prayer Book in Cornwall in 1549; as a member of

---

* See page 122.

† Sumptuary Laws: enacted in the early 15th century to prevent socially ambitious persons from adopting the dress of their superiors.

the Council of Wales he had been consistently harsh in dealing with malefactors; and as a Justice in his own area of Painswick, he

> caused a gallows to be erected on Sheepscombe Green and made a prison in Painswick to secure all offenders. (He) gave three estates called Gallows-land, one to maintain gallows, the second to keep 2 ladders in readiness, and the third to promote halters . . . and that nothing might be wanting, the tything-man of Sheepscombe was to be hangman and to enjoy an acre of land for the service. (Rudder).

Such avid and ruthless determination to exact the harshest penalties of the law and to ensure that no one escaped them, earned Sir Anthony universal opprobrium.

Except where and when they deemed it necessary, the Tudors did not innovate. The Lord Lieutenant, his deputies and the Justices of the Peace were introduced and set over the traditional agents of local government because the latter were not sufficiently flexible (and in some cases reliable) to meet the demands of the changing times. In Gloucestershire, most important of those who were superseded were the Sheriff and his deputy, and the two Sheriffs of Gloucester city, now left with noticeably attenuated responsibility and authority that by the end of the 16th century were far outweighed by the expenses and demands incurred by holding the office. For those aiming to get a foot on the bottom rung of the ladder leading to public recognition, the shrievalty was a useful start and conveniently only a year in duration, since it was coming to be concerned almost exclusively with the preparation for and conduct of the Assizes, when the royal judges visited the county to hear and determine serious criminal cases: and with the collection of taxes.

Preparation for the Assizes was an onerous task involving the presentment of cases, the assembly of juries and witnesses, and the reception, attendance on and entertainment of the judges while the Assizes lasted. Usual expenses might include payments to trumpeters, bailiffs, stewards, criers, a clerk and a chaplain: the cost of candles for the court, pens, ink and paper: and of food and lodgings at reputable inns for the judges themselves and their attendants. The collection of taxes was an even more unrewarding responsibility. Like some of those who took office in the towns, Sheriffs found themselves saddled with arrears that their predecessors had been unable to collect: or at best, were obliged to render at the Exchequer amounts that fell short of what they themselves were answerable for. The business of collecting taxes was disagreeable and necessarily incurred unpopularity with disgruntled payers who claimed that assessments were unfair (as indeed they sometimes were) and limited their contributions to the minimum that would ensure them against punitive procedures. Although, in the event of difficulty, the Sheriff could call on the

Lord Lieutenant to back his efforts, this would have seemed demeaning for one whose authority in the past had been sufficient in itself to the duties required of it.

One other function remained exclusively in the hands of the Sheriffs. Although it might not occur during their year of office, neverthless these officials attached to the county, and the city of Gloucester, had to be prepared to put all the necessary machinery into action in the event of a Parliamentary election. Ever since the inception of Parliament towards the end of the 13th century, it had been customary for the royal writs summoning members to the Commons to be sent to the Sheriffs of every county, ordering them to fix the day and place of the election: to publish this to all interested parties: and then to conduct the proceedings and announce the results. Inevitably therefore, these officials were in a position to exercise considerable influence over the outcome of elections, and as Neale has shown in *The Elizabethan House of Commons*, they were not slow to take advantage of this when their own interests, or those of a friend or colleague were involved, for instance, by revealing relevant details of the arrangements to only one candidate and his followers, leaving all others in the dark until the last moment, thus making it impossible for any rivals to prepare themselves for action.

Thanks to the Tudor practice of making Parliament a party to all important policy decisions, sessions perforce became more frequent than in previous centuries, so that by the end of the 16th century members of the Commons had acquired valuable experience of working together, important privileges including freedom of speech, and a self-confidence that was to prove fatal to the monarchy in the next century. These men could be accounted representative in so far as they were nearly always closely identified with their locality; and that a majority of them belonged to the landowning gentry and were elected by freeholders of the county emphasised the extent to which society was still largely agricultural. That country gentlemen were often to be found representing the enfranchised boroughs also, is explained partly by their willingness to pay their own expenses during the session, partly by their obvious suitability for the work involved, and partly by their keeness to climb higher up the official ladder. To be a member of Parliament, even more than being a Justice of the Peace or a Sheriff, bespoke the position and prestige of one's family in the community that was the county. And in those days, county was synonymous with country. Those who went up to Westminster believed that by serving the interests of their own community – of Gloucestershire for instance – they were also serving England; and with roots buried in native soil, who could be better equipped to do this?

In spite of the desirability of becoming a member of Parliament, the election of knights to represent the county was rarely contested in

Gloucestershire during the 16th century. The recognition of a kind of hierarchy among the gentry allowed members to be returned unopposed and even to retain their seats through several parliaments. It is not surprising that among these, familiar names appear yet again – Tracy, Hungerford, Wynter, Kingston, Chester and Brydges. In the towns, Cirencester, Gloucester and Bristol, the proceedings at election times were likely to be less smooth. In theory such urban communities were still fiercely independent, jealous where their own interests were concerned and proud of their democratic institutions; but already other considerations were beginning to carry weight with the burgess voters, as for instance the expense of sending one of their own number to Westminster and the material advantage of having someone really influential to represent them. Coinciding with this development was the ambition of landed gentlemen to get into Parliament, so that if faced by an offer or a request from one of these to undertake to represent the town, there was a tendency for the burgesses to agree. Cirencester, newly enfranchised during the 16th century, from the start accepted men from county families as its members. Bristol being large and wealthy, was able to retain its independence, and Gloucester endeavoured to do the same, daring even to refuse the Earl of Leicester in 1584 when he asked to be allowed to nominate one of the borough members. 'I will thank you for it and will appoint a sufficient man and see you discharged of all charges in that behalf. If you will send me the election with a blank, I will put in the name'. In the face of such a confident assumption it must have taken courage on the part of the townsfolk to refuse.

The independence of Gloucester voters was not just threatened from outside, however. In several elections, and especially towards the end of the century, a marked difference of opinion arose between the Mayor and members of the town council and the remainder of the burgesses, as to who was suitable to be considered for election, both sides claiming to stand by the traditional custom of choosing only freemen of the borough as members, though both were willing to bend the rule when it suited their purpose. On the occasion of Leicester's attempted interference, the city officials claimed: 'Experience hath taught us what a difficult thing it hath always been to deal in any matter where the multitude of burgesses have voice'; and certainly they tended to become more and more oligarchical in the conduct of elections, until in 1597 there were indications that members of the town council had arranged affairs in such a way that some voters were not aware that the election was in progress, and even those who were present believed that the issue still remained to be determined, when in fact it had already been settled in the council chamber. Here in a small way was the start of borough 'rottenness', so much condemned in the 'unreformed' House of Commons of the late 18th and early 19th century.

The Curfew Tower and Gaol at Moreton in Marsh.

The Stocks at Stow on the Wold.

Town dwellers were necessarily aware of the existence of authority in the persons of guild and urban officials, and of their democratic rights and responsibilities when called upon to vote, to pay rates and play their part in local activities. By contrast, in the country areas, people must have had few reminders of government and the law. Only freeholders with property worth 40 sh or more a year were entitled to vote and therefore participated in Parliamentary elections. Those liable for taxation or military service received official reminders of these obligations but the purpose of them must have seemed somewhat nebulous and remote. Few people, except for habitual wrongdoers, came into contact with the local Justice of the Peace, save when roads had to be repaired, licences obtained or poor rates rendered, but everyone at some time or another had dealings with his subordinate, the Constable, elected by the community but answerable to the Justice for the detection and reporting of local crime – cases of assault, poaching, burglary, drunkenness, or non-observance of the Sabbath for instance.

The Constable was also responsible for seeing that the Justice's orders were carried out in respect of the upkeep of the roads, punishment of vagrants etc., and for organising the hue and cry when criminals had to be pursued and arrested. As a mark of office he wore a badge and carried a stave, and he had charge of the lock-up, the stocks, ducking-stool and other instruments of punishment. Any empty room or hovel might have to serve as a lock-up and it is rarely possible to locate these now, but the one at Moreton-in-Marsh was under the old Curfew Tower, and that at Stow-on-the-Wold in a cellar next to the old Court House. Pillories and ducking-stools have largely disappeared; stocks abound, though not many that still adorn village greens (as at Stow-on-the-Wold) are the original versions. In contemporary literature, the Constable was often portrayed as a figure of fun, no doubt because of the air of importance he assumed; nevertheless in his locality he was expected to be available at all times to deal with minor affrays and disturbances, and anyone who defied his authority would undoubtedly have earned disapproval: vide Verges in *Much Ado about Nothing*: 'If he will not stand when he is bidden, he is none of the prince's subjects.'

During the 16th century there was a marked increase in independence of attitude and action throughout all ranks of society, the result of the spread of education, greater prosperity and more stable conditions; nevertheless a respect for authority and for those who wielded it remained a characteristic of most people. The necessity for order and degree was emphasised continually in church sermons, Parliamentary speeches, pronouncements made by the sovereign and members of the Privy Council, and in contemporary writings. The famous speech in *Troilus and Cressida* would not have caused surprise nor provoked arguments since it merely expressed sentiments that were widely held and respected:

Thomas Dutton, Sheriff of Gloucestershire in the 16th century.

The heavens themselves, the planets and the centre
Observe degree, priority and place . . .
O when degree is shaked,
Which is the ladder to all high designs,
The enterprise is sick. . . .

The lively interest in education which followed the arrival of Renaissance influences in England led to a new emphasis on the preparation of young men for a career, whether it was apprentices for a craft, the sons of merchants for a share in the family business, young gentlemen and nobles for posts of responsibility in connection with the Church, the law or government. It was with the latter in view that books such as Roger Ascham's *The Scholemaster* and Thomas Elyot's *The Governour* were written and that William Cecil started his household school for wards of court, in order to emphasise that future governors should have not just book learning but also qualities of character deserving of the respect given to public figures. Having passed through the hands of schoolmasters or private tutors, and proceeded to University or the Inns of Court, it was now considered useful

Richard Pate, Recorder of Gloucester.

if not essential for a young man to travel abroad 'to furnish himself with the knowledge of such things as may be serviceable to his country', which were to include not just foreign languages and customs, but also riding, tennis, dancing and fencing as taught by leading experts in France and Italy. The growing importance of travel is reflected in a letter from Sir Christopher Hatton to Thomas Dutton of Sherborne, who had requested permission for his son to go abroad:

> Her Majesty doth very graciously accept of the gentleman's travel with assurance that he will prove a man meet to be hereafter employed in service for the benefit of his country.

Whatever their background and training, the men who assumed responsibility for local and national administration were all imbued with a willingness to serve and a tolerant understanding of their fellow men that enabled them to deal firmly and sympathetically with whatever problems they were faced with – whether it was the collection of taxes, an increase in the number of vagrants on the roads, or a parliamentary bill affecting trade or industry. That the same names recurred generation after generation in the lists of Justices, Sheriffs and Members of Parliament for Gloucestershire – Dutton, Brydges, Wynter, Estcourt, Guise, Leigh, Kingston, Tracy, Hungerford – indicated that their capacity for service was an inherited one and expected of such families. Nor was it peculiar to the landed gentry. Merchant families in the towns produced men of similar character who gave generously of their time, energies and charity while they were in office as Aldermen, Councillors or Mayors. Some of them also achieved posts in London as did Richard Pate, but he returned to his home county in due course to act as Recorder of Gloucester and become the benefactor of the poor and needy there and in Cheltenham, his birthplace, where he arranged for 'the perpetual maintenance and foundation of a free Grammar School – and also a Hospital or Almshouse for six old poor people'.

Thus the Parliaments, Councils and Judicature under the Tudors were filled with men of varying abilities, interests and standing but similar loyalty and usefulness, according to Henry VIII's pronouncement that he would be served by men 'of what degree soever'. Bearing this out and illustrating that in the 16th century careers were indeed open to talent, is the case of Robert Willis of Gloucester who was educated at the free Grammar School there, and 'though I were no graduate of the University yet I had so much learning as fitted me for the places whereunto the Lord advanced me', which in his case included the secretaryship to the Chancellor of the Exchequer, Lord High Treasurer of England and the Lord Keeper of the Great Seal. That particular local boy certainly made good.

7
Alarms and Excursions

'What folly, what madness is this, to make a hole in the ship thou sailest in.'

As compared with other countries in Europe, England was markedly peaceful and stable during the 16th century. France, the Low Countries, Germany, Italy and Spain were fought over by foreign armies and torn by domestic strife, so that everywhere lives were being lost, goods and money wastefully expended, economic life disrupted, and the morale of the people destroyed. However, it must not be assumed that this country was entirely without problems and consequent disturbances, or that there were no differences of opinion and outlook among its citizens. It was just that England was protected from land invasion by its insular position, and had a government so carefully attuned to public feeling that – except under Mary – it could steer clear of fervent extremes and follow a policy designed to appeal to the majority of people, who were usually more anxious to continue in their accustomed way of life than to abandon it in search of some ideal, inspiring perhaps, but by no means certainly attainable. Even the most adventurous and enterprising Englishman in the 16th century was a realist at heart!

Generally speaking, both underlying unrest and overt rebellion in England during the Tudor period were the response of local communities to local grievances. Only rarely was the Crown itself or its policies challenged, for therein lay the chief safeguard of the country against civil war. 'Ye resist your king if ye resist his proceeding' wrote Udall, to bring home the meaning of treason as interpreted by Henry VIII and his successors. However, it was an indication of increasing awareness of governmental encroachment into local affairs, that as the 16th century progressed, ordinary people were readier to hold officialdom responsible for their grievances regardless of the fact that many current problems were both unprecedented and complex, defying easy diagnosis and instant solution, and moreover were created by forces not just local or national but European.

On the whole Gloucestershire was less troubled than many parts of

Bishop John Hooper: executed at Gloucester in 1554.

England, because until this time the county had been a border area affording a peaceful no-man's land between England and what was still regarded as 'the wilds of Wales.' Influential men here, though a few might quarrel with each other, had managed to remain aloof from national politics except in so far as they served as Sheriffs, Justices of the Peace or members of Parliament: and meanwhile ordinary folk proceeded to make a success of their work on the land or as urban craftsmen and traders, so it was only when official policy or particular local circumstances threatened the even tenor of their lives that they were stirred to action. Elsewhere, changes in religion might provoke pilgrimage or petition: heavy taxation riotous remonstrance: and food shortages violent attacks on suspected hoarders and profiteers: but in Gloucestershire it was a minority that actively opposed official policy during the Reformation, resisted demands for taxes or resorted to self-help in times of want. Political issues, such as challenges to the succession, merited mere passing attention in borough records:

> Paid to him that brought the proclamacion for Lady Jane . . .
> Given to the gentilman that browghte the proclamacion for the Queen's Grace that nowe is . . .
> Given to him that browght the newes that Wyatt was takyn . . .

Bishop Hooper's Lodging at Gloucester.

Enclosures, mostly made by agreement among yeoman farmers, did not, as elsewhere, create the twin grievances of depopulation and impoverishment: and only the threat of invasion in 1588 roused the whole of the county to action – but on the side of the government and not against it.

As has been shown in an earlier chapter, until the reign of Mary (1553–1558) the full impact of what was happening to the church in England was not felt sharply by the people in Gloucestershire, partly because they were prepared for change by the inherited influence of Lollardy, and partly because priests and people understood each other and together adapted – as gently as possible – to each new development as it came along. The material changes that followed the dissolution of the monasteries and chantry chapels, and the removal of 'Popish' furnishings and decorations from church interiors undoubtedly meant more to the uneducated than any doctrinal reform, which few understood anyway. Indeed, in this sphere 'the sincere word of God set forth by the King's Majesty' as recommended to them for acceptance by their parish priests, must have seemed much more nearly within their grasp than the mysteries of the Roman Catholic faith. It needed the persecution that began under Mary to bring home to those hitherto little affected, their unavoidable involvement in national events.

Of notable people in Gloucestershire, Bishop Hooper was the only one to suffer. After being condemned for his refusal to recant Protestant doctrines and return to the Catholic faith and usages, he was taken back to Gloucester where he was burned 'for the example and terror of others such as he hath there seduced and mistaught'. Whether they grieved in private for him is not known, but the members of his flock who had looked up to him as their shepherd were not noticeably stirred by his death, while those in charge of the execution proceedings seem to have treated it as just another civic duty:

> 'Money given in reward to the Kynge and Queenes servauntes at the bryngyng down of Maister Hooper to be brente: for a diner made and gevyn to the Lord Chandos and other gentlemen at Maister Maires house that day that Maister Hooper was brant.

Of the other ten martyrs in the county little is known save that they were of humble origin like so many of the victims of Mary's religious zeal. They included a bricklayer, a carpenter, a shepherd, a blind boy and several women, all of whom were condemned for the heresy of refusing to believe in Transubstantiation, the full implication of which must surely have been beyond their comprehension. That their deaths were accepted with equanimity by their friends and neighbours seems more likely due to the general acceptance of governmental authority and action than to any positive desire for a return to Catholicism. It is noticeable also that priests who had taken advantage of Edwardian dispensations and married, were now prepared to set aside their wives rather than lose their livings: and the willingness of both clerics and congregations to toe the official line is further proved by entries in parish records at the time, which show that items of church plate, missals, vestments and crosses were hidden during the reign of Edward VI, brought out again and used under Mary, only to disappear for a second time when the Elizabethan Church Settlement was established.

The arrangements made about religion within a year of Elizabeth's accession in 1558 constituted a compromise – a via media between the courses that had been taken during the three previous reigns – and were intended to salve the consciences and feelings of all those who had suffered as the pendulum swung from moderate to extreme reform under Henry VIII and Edward VI and then back again to equally extreme reactionary measures under Mary. They did not represent the Queen's personal religious convictions which – except in her stated preference for a celibate clergy and dignified ritualistic services – she successfully kept to herself; but they did reflect what she believed would be acceptable to the majority of her people. Acquiescence in the Royal Supremacy over church government, the use of the English Prayer Book and regular attendance at its services were required of the laity, while the Royal Injunctions (also issued in 1559) were directed at the bishops, making regular visitations of their dioceses obliga-

Northleach: Chalice dated 1569.

tory so that they might ensure the people's acceptance of the Acts of
Supremacy and Uniformity, together with the willingness and diligence of
the clergy to see that their congregations not merely conformed in practice
to the terms of the settlement but also grasped the political and spiritual
significance of them.

But, as in earlier reigns, however assiduous the bishops might be, the
extent and effectiveness of their authority depended largely on the calibre of
the parish clergy, many of whom still lacked the scholarship and missionary
zeal to form a spear-head of influence, so until the wider spread of education
provided more suitable candidates for ordination, official requirements
were by no means fully met. Episcopal visitations revealed many
shortcomings among the clergy – ignorance, indifference and absenteeism –
which may have left the congregations free to think and act much as they
liked, but did not encourage their commitment to particular doctrines and
usages. For twenty years of the reign the see of Gloucester suffered not only
from inefficient lesser clergy, but also from outstanding incompetence on

the part of its bishop Richard Cheyney, and the blatant greed and corruption of the chancellor of the diocese Thomas Powell, so that where genuine pastoral care prevailed it was thanks to the concern of a particular priest, and not to his superiors. Under the circumstances, it is surprising that most of the laity did not become as indifferent to their religious responsibilities as their mentors, but this was not the case. Even before governmental regulations were tightened, church going continued as a regular habit; money was forthcoming for church repairs, for pulpits and pews, (necessitated by compulsory sermons) for new articles of plate for use in the Communion service where the congregation now participated; and the bequests of parishioners, instead of being left for altar candles and prayers for the dead, might be for the expenses of a preacher or for copies of the Bible and Prayer Books.

Inevitably, like all compromises, Elizabeth's via media had only limited success since the consciences of those well to the left and right of centre would not allow them to accept it. The inheritors of Lollard traditions who had welcomed the move towards a Bible and Prayer Book in English and less ritualistic services, and been obliged to leave the country or hold their peace during the Catholic reaction of Mary's reign, hoped to see a further advance under Elizabeth towards the banning of clerical vestments, the simplification of services and an end to all 'superstitious' observances and practices. They would even have had that most characteristic sound of the English countryside – the ringing of church bells – silenced for ever. Although they were strengthened in their convictions by the return of exiles from abroad imbued with German and Swiss ideas of reform, these English Protestants failed to convert the Queen to their point of view, so from the early years of the reign overt disapproval of her religious settlement became their policy.

In Gloucestershire, where the views of many people tended to favour change and reform, the Puritans were not regarded with as much hostility as in some places. Lack of supervision from above and the close affinity of parson and congregation which often existed in country areas, meant that official regulations were interpreted according to the wishes of each particular congregation, a mixture of traditional and innovatory features usually ensuing; but in the towns, always to the fore where new ideas were concerned, Puritanism was uniformly popular and widespread. Civic officials on public occasions upheld the letter of the law and attended services in urban churches that conformed in every way to the requirements of the Act of Uniformity and the Royal Injunctions. At the same time they sanctioned the employment of 'preachers' to implement the work of clergy found wanting in this respect, and only when the former expressed views that verged on sedition or attempted to hold irregular services outside the churches, were they frowned upon. In the larger towns and more important market centres, the hard-working enterprising and often self-righteous bourgeoisie asserted their independence by espousing theological views which put a seal of approval on their economic activities – namely that God looked favourably on the industrious, the thrifty and those who were zealous in religious observance. Usually tolerated, they were neverthless recognised as a potential source of trouble, as at Cirencester, where they were 'proof against all authority: a sect of disordered persons using to assemble together in a desolate place nere unto a woodeside appointing unto themselves a minister and a private Order of Service according to their own fantasies.'

As the next century was to prove, and as Elizabeth herself recognised ('I must pronounce them dangerous to a kingly rule') the Protestant non-conformists, whose religious views soon became inseparable from political ambitions, were potentially the more threatening of the two extreme parties which refused to accept the Elizabethan Church Settlement. At the time, however, it was the Catholics who were most feared, partly because – even if not in Gloucestershire – a majority of people tended to cling to traditional practices, and partly because after the excommunication of Elizabeth by Pope Pius V in 1570, allegiance to Catholicism began to be equated with un-English proclivities and even treason. Until this point, known Catholics had been accepted and respected members of society (they mostly belonged to the gentry and aristocracy) but the Pope's pronouncement and the Queen's retaliatory measures made it impossible for Catholics to continue compromising as they had done so far, by remaining loyal in spirit to their sovereign while conforming in as few ways as possible to her religious settlement. They had been able to do this because some were magistrates empowered to execute the new laws at their own discretion, and many had private chapels where Catholic services could be celebrated after token appearances had been made at the local parish church. However, after 1570, Recusancy Laws imposed fines of increasing severity on those who did not attend church services, banned such people from holding public office and in time curtailed even their social freedom by prohibiting them to travel without a licence. To remain in communication with the Roman church either by correspondence or through the services of a Catholic priest, became a treasonable offence.

To enforce these laws and indeed to counter any threats to the Queen's authority in ecclesiastical matters, special commissions answerable to the Privy Council were set up. They worked on an itinerant basis in different parts of the country and consisted of episcopal officers, lay magistrates and local magnates. The commission for the western counties included well-known Gloucestershire names – Tracey, Pate, Dutton, Berkeley and Brydges. Sir Giles Brydges, Lord Lieutenant of the County, and warden of Sudeley Castle, was most assiduous in fulfilling his responsibilities, and whether he was presiding in person over the court or not, exercised a considerable influence over the other commissioners, a measure of his standing with the Queen and of his authority locally. The Commission Court met at Gloucester, Painswick, Wotton-under-Edge, Sapperton, Cirencester, Tewkesbury and elsewhere, dealing with complaints referred to it by the Justices of the Peace, episcopal officials, churchwardens and disgruntled members of the public; and usually by sentencing offenders to the pillory, the stocks, a whipping or penitential appearance in church and the market square, the commissioners succeeded in confining laity and clergy to the middle way, and as far as Catholics were concerned, by the 1590's, had reduced the number of known recusants to 20, among whom were members of the Pauncefoot family, ultimately so impoverished by fines that they had to sell their home, Hasfield Court. Priests sent from seminaries abroad to keep the Catholic faith alive here in England met with much harsher treatment. Five were caught in Gloucestershire, and of these two died in prison and three were executed, two at Gloucester in particularly horrific circumstances for which Sir Giles Brydges and Paul Tracy were largely responsible. How many secret adherents of the old faith remained is impossible to assess. A few local families had marriage connections – and presumably sympathy – with Catholics outside the county, and we are reminded that Catholic tendencies died hard when early in the next reign the epithet 'Popish' was frequently used to describe those who did not share the views of their more Puritanically inclined brethren.

Thus religion, though a matter of concern, never became a major source of unrest and contention in Gloucestershire during the 16th century, and even serious upheavals elsewhere – the Pilgrimage of Grace in 1536 and the Western Rising against the Prayer Book in 1549 – failed to raise any sympathetic interest here. Other national problems did affect the county. These were the evils of poverty, unemployment and consequent vagrancy.

Poverty, an ever-present factor in the community, reached unprecedented proportions during the 16th century for a number of reasons. In the first place, the steady rise in population increased proportionately the number of poor, and similarly more people were affected by fluctuations in trade and industry which caused distress among those dependent on them for employment and subsistence: and by bad harvests which affected the food supplies of town and country dwellers alike. Then inflation, due to the demand for goods out-stripping supply and aggravated by increasing governmental expenditure, was made considerably worse instead of being cured (as was hoped) by debasements of the coinage under Henry VIII and Edward VI. And just when they were most needed, some traditional sources of alms – the monasteries, chantry chapels and charity bestowed by individuals – came to an end with the Reformation.

The Chandos Almshouses at Winchcombe founded in 1573.

Poverty and unemployment went hand in hand and together formed a vicious spiral in which men were caught inescapably. Without work, they could not hope to have an independent means of subsistence; without money, they could not afford to rent land or pay for fools, materials and other means of making a livelihood. Those who seriously wanted to work along with those determined not to do so, took to the roads – the first in the hope of finding more favourable circumstances somewhere on their route, the second to avoid committing themselves to responsibilities in any fixed place. Gloucestershire, because of its healthy agriculture and flourishing trade tended generally to have no more than a hard core of indigenous poor. In other parts of the country, the enclosure of open fields and common land was responsible for unemployment among cottage dwellers, but this was not true of a county where well–run monastic estates were now in the hands of capable lay owners, and where both pastoral and arable farming was a source of profit. Admittedly, if there was a slump in the cloth trade, the lowest paid workers were the first to feel the pinch since the clothiers immediately stopped distributing wool to the cottagers for spinning and thus deprived the weavers of supplies also; but seemingly hopeful on these occasions of a future improvement in their fortunes, Gloucestershire workers were not goaded into violent action as for instance the people of East Anglia in 1529, when

> The clothiers all, not able to maintain
> The many to them 'longing, have put off
> The spinsters, carders, fullers, weavers who
> Unfit for other life, compelled by hunger
> And lack of other means, in desperate manner
> Daring the event to the teeth, are all in uproar.

Because of its geographical position astride the routes between the south-western counties and the Midlands, Wales and the Thames Valley, Gloucestershire acquired during the 16th century some of the destitute of other regions as well, who either came here in search of work or passed through in search of more promising areas beyond. Thus to local unsettled elements was added an alien one, which – as far as the authorities were concerned – rendered the situation dangerous and called for restrictive measures. We have noticed how the towns responded to this situation by appointing Beadles of the Beggars to deter vagrants from lingering in the area and making importunate demands on worthy citizens meanwhile, and the alien element among the intruders is indicated by the many references to 'Egyptians'. 'For byrche to make roddes to beat the Egypcyans naked about the citie; for the cart whereat the said Egypcyans were tyed and so brought about the citie and scourged.' While thus distancing themselves from the plight of the stranger, the towns were neverthless ahead of other areas in devising means of helping their indigenous poor. To fill the gap caused by the dissolution of the monasteries and chantries, which had been dispensers of charity during the Middle Ages, there appeared in due course almshouses and hospitals financed either by civic authorities or individuals, to provide shelter and care for the needy, infirm and aged. Northleach, Winchcombe, Tewkesbury and Gloucester among other places acquired such institutions which were supported not only with money from bequests and civic funds, but also gifts in kind from merchants and tradesmen. Joan Goldston of Gloucester by her will left 'twenty pounds for the provision of wood and coal, together with money for wood as fuel for the inhabitants of St. Bartholomew's Hospital', and it has been suggested that as her husband was in the timber trade, this bequest was merely the continuation of a practice begun during their life times, of distributing wood as fuel to those who needed it.* If the poor were not infirm, to stave off the need for a compulsory levy to support them, they might be allowed to beg, and Gloucester was one of the earliest towns in the country to issue badges to those thus licensed, as the borough records show: 'Paid for making of a molde for the beggars' bages, and pewter and workmanship of same.'

---

* Frith: *Twelve Portraits of Gloucester Benefactors.*

Gloucester: St Bartholomew's Hospital.

The problems of poverty, unemployment and vagrancy were not peculiar to Gloucestershire. They were indeed much more serious elsewhere, and by the middle of the 16th century had become a nation-wide issue that demanded governmental attention and led to the passing of a series of Poor Laws designed to stop these troubles at source, by making every parish responsible for its own poor. Initially it was the threat to public order posed by the movement through the countryside of rootless and often lawless persons, that most concerned the authorities, and explained the severity of the statutes up to Elizabeth's reign. The law of 1547 was particularly savage in its penalties for vagrancy and unlicensed begging – whipping, branding and death being advocated for repeated offences. Under Elizabeth however, a more humane attitude was shown in that a distinction was made between the impotent poor for whom shelter and care were to be provided, the able-bodied unemployed for whom work was to be found, and the determined idlers who were to be put in a House of Correction or gaoled. Justices of the Peace, or Overseers of the Poor appointed by them, worked hand in hand with churchwardens to distribute the funds now raised from a compulsory poor rate on all churchgoers and fines imposed for non-attendance at church. The various laws passed during the reign and finally codified between 1598 and 1601 were considered

Joan Goldston, a Gloucester benefactress.

enlightened for their time and put England ahead of the rest of Europe in social welfare; and while increasingly inadequate in the face of a rapid rise in population during the late 18th century and early 19th century, and the unprecedented problems caused by the industrial changes of that time, they remained in force until the New Poor Law was introduced in 1834.

As with all administrative measures, the effectiveness of the Poor Laws depended largely on the conscientiousness of those entrusted with enforcing them. In the towns, the jealous protection of citizens' rights, employment and property led to a fairly intransigent attitude towards outsiders who ventured there in search of work or charity, and one wonders whether it was because the Beadle was negligent or the vagrant incursors so numerous, that the Gloucester Borough Records noted: 'The Beadle is to have 12d from the steward for every rogue or vagrant person that he shall whip and is sent away with a pass according to the Statute; and 6d for every vagrant taken up and committed to the Bridewell.' In the countryside, where the problem was not so serious anyway, country folk being more self-sufficient than townsmen, Justices and Overseers were inclined to temper justice with a degree of mercy, and while speeding strangers on their way to their own parishes, often did so with a gift of money or perhaps the help of some means of transport.

During the latter part of the 16th century, vagrancy was a mounting threat to law and order; poverty in itself was not, except when bad harvests led to food shortages and sparked off illegal practices such as hoarding, forestalling and regrating on the part of dealers anxious to force prices upwards. People in the towns, almost entirely dependent on bought supplies of food, were most severely affected by rising prices, but even the users of country markets might suffer. These were the occasions when 'authority' was expected to take action, and indeed Justices of the Peace did their best to hold prices at a reasonable level and to punish anyone who tried to get round their ruling. The following account of a food riot in Gloucester in 1586, a particularly bad harvest year, reflects growing popular concern at the engrossment of barley supplies by brewers, the importance of the Severn as a highway for traffic in grain, and the close links between Gloucestershire and London:

> This year about Easter, great numbers of weavers, tuckers and other persons most poor and some wealthy, assembled themselves at Severn side and there stopped a boat laden with malt passing down Severn to serve North Wales, and rifled, spoiled and took away the malt against the wish of the owners, and in great disorder demeaned themselves. And afterwards, a boat laden with malt for a brewer of Bristol, in like sort. And so the passage of corn down the Severn was stayed for a season. During the most part of the summer, corn continued at great and high prices notwithstanding all the policy and consultation taken against the same. This extremity remained more in the County of Gloucester than in any other shire adjoining save in Bristol where for a space they were hard distressed, but the great plenty of corn that came to London from Denmark, Hamburg and other places beyond the seas kept down the price: and from thence good store came to Bristol, part thereof was gotten hither from thence and so provision was made from London to Gloucester.*

Some years later in 1595 and 1597 there was further trouble:

> Grain was so high before the harvest that proclamations were published to restrain the prices to the rates they were at 2 months before, which even so were excessive considering the shortage of money. During these times, the citizens of Gloucester stretched a chain across the Severn that no vessels with provisions might pass beyond them; but the town of Tewkesbury petitioning the Privy Council, they caused the chain to be taken down.

* Rudder: *A New History of Gloucestershire.*

Tewkesbury: a rival port to Gloucester on the River Severn.

The record continues: 'Pestilence commonly succeeds to famine', and this was the other misfortune that people viewed with alarm during the 16th century. In Gloucestershire the worst outbreaks of plague seem to have occurred towards the end of the century, especially in the towns where because of in-filling and the subdivision of houses in the poorer quarters, more crowded conditions existed, so that more people were living in insalubrious circumstances. During an outbreak in Tewkesbury in 1591, all markets and fairs were cancelled and 'numbers would have perished if well-disposed persons in the neighbourhood had not sent provisions and money to the poor in the town'. The outbreak in 1598 was not so serious, but another in 1602 caused 500 deaths, and in 1604 'the plague broke out again. It was occasioned by some trowmen of the town bringing it from Bristol. 23 persons died of it, all of whom to avoid peril were buried in coffins of wood'. It is not surprising that whenever cases of plague were reported in the neighbourhood, town authorities took action to discourage any kind of gatherings that might attract strangers.

Finally, among potential causes of alarm as the century drew to a close was the question of national security. This would not have concerned the average citizen a hundred years earlier, when those who could remember the Wars of the Roses were inclined to put the safety of person and property before all else. But by the end of the century, thanks to the policy of the Tudors which had exalted nationalism as a matter of political expediency and as an inspiration, many people were conscious and proud of being

English, and were even capable of putting the country's interests before their own. As we have seen, crises over the succession or of rebellion in other parts of the country, affected people in Gloucestershire very little, but the imminence of war with Spain as the reign of Elizabeth progressed, touched them more nearly, since much of the county's prosperity was now bound up with trade in the Channel and the estuary of the Severn, and any circumstance that threatened to interrupt this, was recognised as potentially dangerous. So as the nation drifted nearer to the brink of war between 1586 and 1588, there was no popular objection to Gloucestershire being put into a state of preparedness. Musters of men and supplies of arms were assembled for inspection by the Lord Lieutenant or his subordinates: towns repaired their defences: beacons were placed on hilltops with men ready to fire them in the event of an enemy force being sighted at sea: and only a single church bell summoned the faithful to church each Sunday so that the ringing of a full peal would serve as an effective alarm signal.

Unlike other contemporary European rulers, the Tudors had no standing army to use in cases of emergency; they relied instead on all men between 16 and 60 years of age to take up arms and rally to the defence of the country. Wealthy individuals, along with towns and villages, were expected to provide arms, armour and ammunition, also coats for the men to wear. If the crisis required the men to move away from home and outside their own county, then they were paid. Ports on the Severn provided ships as well as men for defence purposes. The townsfolk of Tewkesbury paid for a ship to be 'rigged and stocked with victuals for 3 months to prepare against the Armada' and together with the citizens of Gloucester they furnished and manned a pinnace with a crew equipped and ready to sail it. As far as defence was concerned, Gloucestershire had an added responsibility, namely the Forest of Dean which was the chief source of timber for England's naval vessels and a particular target for Spain's hostile intentions if the following story told by Wantner is to be believed:

> The Spaniards in the reign of Queen Elizabeth sent over an ambassador of purpose into England to try if he could either by private practices, great rewards, fair promises or any other contrivances whatsoever, procure this wooden wall, the strength of our kingdom, to be distroyed; who, had he effected his master's commission, had right well his particular favour.

The part played by Gloucestershire men during the Armada crisis is related in the Gloucester Borough Records:

> Upon the descrying of the Spanish fleet near Plymouth the 20th day of July 1588, special word came to the Lord Lieutenant for the present arming and setting forth of 1500 men to be brought to London out of

Militiamen: a pikeman and a musketeer.

the Lieutenancy, whereupon there was a meeting at Ciceter by many of the muster . . . The soldiers of the cyttie and libertee marched on Satterday the third of August to Fairford to bedd and from thence on the Sunday to Dorchester and Abingdon and from thence on the Monday the 5th of August to the elm park where their captain mustered them before the old Lady Chandos; and before two of the clock on that Monday, tidings came from Sir Henry Poole that he had received special worde from the privie Counsaile that all the captains with their bands should returne back into their countries and discharge their soldiers; whereupon the Lieutenant led his soldiers to Ciceter homeward where they were discharged.

When it became known that 'the Spanish fleet had been fought with at the bay near Calais and there lost one of their greatest Armadas', the Lord Lieutenant ordered his deputies to ensure 'the safe keeping of the swords, daggers, belts and girdles of every man and of the greatest number of the coats'. However it was subsequently discovered that some of the arms stored at Winchcombe just disappeared, while those 'placed by special order of the Lord Lieutenant in the Bartholomew Hall in Gloucester . . . were somehow changed and worse left in their place'.

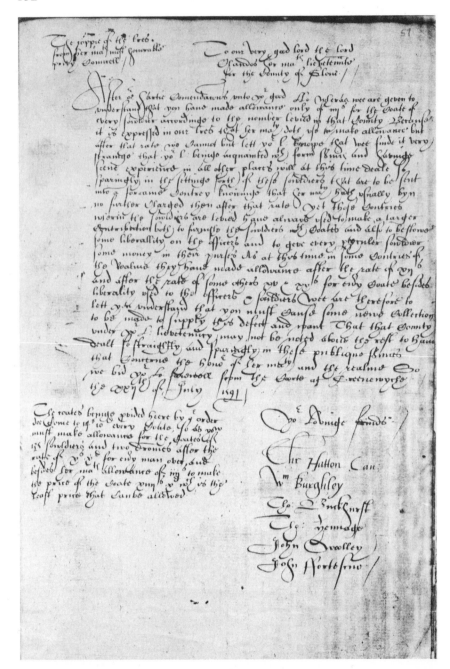

A reprimand from the Royal Council to the Lord Lieutenant.

These last two occurrences throw light on a common practice among the militia men of the time who considered that they were underpaid and therefore entitled to exploit any opportunities for making money. Thus some sold their arms, especially muskets which were not easy to come by; while others exchanged inferior weapons for something better. The matter of the provision of coats gave rise to a contretemps between the Lord Lieutenant and the Privy Council three years later when men were again needed, this time for service in France. Although it was understood that each county should bear the cost of coats for the militia (15 shillings each) the government in fact contributed 4 shillings towards this. Lord Chandos suggested that it was unfair for the county to have to subscribe more than an equal amount, thus provoking the Privy Council into sending him a sharp reprimand. He knew that it was the general practice for the county to provide the bulk of the money for coats: indeed some counties not only did this but also gave both officers and men something for their own purses. He was therefore ordered 'to supply this defect and want', so that the county under his lieutenancy 'may not be noted above the rest to have dealt so straightly and sparingly in these publique affairs that concern the honour of Her Majesty and the realme.'

It would seem that on this occasion, in contrast with earlier enthusiasm for opposing the Armada, the Lord Lieutenant came up against opposition in the county to any further contributions to the war effort. However, it is perhaps relevant to recall that throughout the century Gloucestershire had been the main recruiting ground when troops were needed for service in Ireland, and had supplied more men than any other county for this purpose, while its overall contribution in terms of money, men and arms for service overseas was also, except for London, Kent and Essex, the highest in the country. When times were bad, as they were in the 1590's, because of food shortages and poverty, the people were least co-operative and inclined to make demands of the government rather than have it make demands of them. The defeat of the Armada had been the climax of a century of national progress; no further efforts should be required or expected of those who had helped to put England in the forefront of European countries.

8
Pleasures and Pastimes

'The English are naturally inclined to pleasure . . .'

Alone of European countries during the 16th century, England experienced a period of stability and increasing prosperity that boosted popular morale and encouraged the exploitation of every opportunity that occurred for relaxation and enjoyment. Such a feeling of confidence in both the present and the future was a measure of the success of Tudor government. During the early part of the period, when people could still remember the insecurity and terrors of civil war, the advantages of the present over the past were such as to incline men to regard the monarchy (which after all was at the heart of government) as the source and guarantee of their enjoyment of life. Later on, in Elizabeth's reign, when the peace of the country was threatened once more, this time by Catholic plots at home and invasion from abroad, the same trust in the sovereign inspired national confidence and resolution, and helped to ensure ultimate triumph in the face of these dangers.

As in the serious business of politics, so in the more light-hearted pursuit of pleasure, the English people in the 16th century looked to their sovereigns to set new fashions or to show their approval of established practices. Although better educated and more aesthetically aware than the majority of their subjects, and capable of distancing themselves from the masses when political expediency demanded, the Tudors were able and willing on occasion to take pleasure in many of the popular pastimes of the day. Henry VII when not weighed down by the cares of government, liked to watch bear-baiting, cock-fighting, wrestling, tumblers and jugglers; and during his visit to Gloucester in 1486, 'though there was no pageaunt nor speche ordeynde', he watched – along with the townsfolk – processions of churchmen and civic dignitaries clad in rich and colourful clothes. Henry VIII, as well as excelling in the practice of all outdoor sports, was a skilled musician and was accompanied by his own players and band of trumpeters when travelling. (The latter received gratuities when the King visited Gloucester in 1535). His daughter Mary also appreciated music, and while she was a guest of the abbot of Tewkesbury in 1525, the latter ordered 'Trumpets and rebecks to be sent to provide for interludes,

Map of the Cotswolds from Michael Drayton's Polyolbion.

disguisings and plays, and for the banquet on Twelfth Night'. Elizabeth who, surrounded by her court, took pleasure in plays, dancing, music, hunting and riding, could also sit through the spontaneous amateur performances that were inevitable features of her progresses through the countryside, and seemingly share the enjoyment of local bystanders in displays of rustic wit and unsophisticated merrymaking.

Of course, except for the wealthy, no one in the 16th century had leisure in the sense and to the degree that we do today; neverthless in all classes – given the opportunity – there was an immediate response to music, unusual sights and occasions for celebration, doubtless because for those who had to earn their living, hours of work were long and conditions demanding, so that as much enjoyment as possible had to be crowded into periods of respite. 'Merrie England' was an apt description of the towns on fair days, when rich and poor alike rubbed shoulders in the market place, laughed together at the antics of clowns, ate spiced gingerbread and hot pies, and shared the excitement when a dancing bear appeared; or of the country villages on May Day, when the young rose early to collect leaves and flowers to deck themselves and their homes, and later danced round the Maypole watched by their elders: while as the day advanced, more and

A Royal Picnic: from Turberville's Booke of Hunting.

more people resorted to the village inn for refreshment and indulged in
bouts of cudgelling, fisticuffs or wrestling.

For the rich, leisure was never in short supply; indeed at times the
problem must have been to find ways of filling the hours between dawn and
sunset, if official calls on time or the care of a household and an estate were
not sufficient. Although their homes were furnished with all the comforts
available at the time, and frequently had long galleries where exercise could
be taken, nevertheless the wealthy tended to get their pleasure from outdoor
activities – hunting, coursing, falconry and archery – the first of which at
any rate involved long hours of riding in all weathers. It was taken for
granted that men of means would have horses, dogs and the necessary
equipment to enable them to indulge in all kinds of sport: nor was it

surprising that, if they could afford, like Henry Lord Berkeley they would seek the best:

> 'His chiefe delights wherein he spent neare three parts of the yeare, were to his great charges, in hunting the hare, fox and deere, red and fallow, not wanting choice of as good hunting horses as yearly hee could buy at faires in the North; And in hawking both at river and at land: And as his hounds were held inferior to no mans, soe were his hawks of severall sorts; which if he sent not a man to fetch from beyond seas, yet had hee the choice as soone as they were brought over into England, keeping a man lodging in London to bee sure of his choice at their first landing; especially for his haggard falcons for the river . . . that were famous with all great faulconers in many countries.'*

During the Middle Ages the monarchs had set a fashion in their fondness for hunting, and one reason for the royal partiality towards Gloucestershire had been its admirable hunting grounds. Indeed until the late 17th century there was a royal 'Keeper of Game for His Majesty's Disport and Recreation' in Gloucestershire, Worcestershire and Herefordshire, Wales and the Marches.

According to Leland, already by the 16th century 'every considerate landowner had his paled park and often two, one for red and one for fallow deer'; and during the course of the century some of these existing ones were enlarged and many more made. As well as important properties such as Berkeley, Badminton, Sherborne and Sudeley, lesser ones were similarly equipped – Ampney Crucis, Barnsley, Fairford, Rendcomb, Southam and Batsford which had 'a small but beautiful and well ordered park of about 95 acres with 200 fallow deer'. For both the participants and onlookers the practice of outdoor sports and its associated vocabulary was very much a part of everyday life. Clearly in response to interest and demand, two books were published in 1575 and 1576, Turberville's *Booke of Hunting* and *Booke of Falconrie* describing the 'art' of these sports and illustrated with drawings showing how weapons should be handled and what dress should be worn. The use of sporting terms in contemporary literature implied that an acquaintance with and understanding of these could bestow a certain cachet: 'An a man have not skill in the hawking and hunting language, I'll not give a rush for him'. (Ben Jonson).

To those excluded from the hunting parties, the emparking of land was not always regarded with favour. For instance, fences might not be adequate to confine the deer which could and did escape to do harm to trees and growing crops outside the park; and sometimes the land enclosed to make a park had formerly been common pasture or arable, so that the pleasure of a few was achieved at the expense of many. When the Duke of Buckingham was building his mansion at Thornbury and surrounded it

* Smith: *Lives of the Berkeleys.*

Correct Sporting Outfit: from Turberville's Booke of
Falconrie.

with a park, it was reported: 'The inhabitants cursyd the Duke for their
lands so inclosyd'. Nevertheless for the most part the sporting activities of
the wealthy were recognised as a source of extra employment for local
inhabitants as well as an exciting spectacle of well-dressed riders, fine horses
and dogs, and elaborate al-fresco meals set out and eaten before the hunt
began and during the course of the day. Fowling and fishing, popular sports
elsewhere, were not so widely practised in Gloucestershire, although the
Severn and tributaries of the Thames were well stocked with fish and the
banks of the Severn offered the right conditions for fowling. Undoubtedly
the less wealthy exploited these means to supplement their larders, but that
they were also enjoyed by their betters is indicated in a deed dated 1582,
which conveyed to Sir Walter Raleigh the right to hunt in the park of
Badminton Manor, also, 'the title to fishing, fowling, hawking and
hunting.'

Another, gentler, outdoor activity, increasingly popular among the
wealthy during the 16th century, was the making of gardens. 'The English
are so naturally inclined to pleasure as there is no country where all sorts of

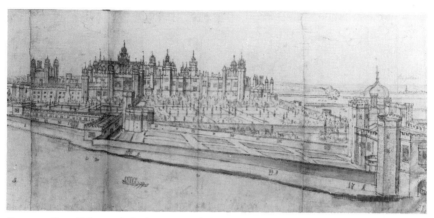

Hampton Court Palace and Gardens: a model for 16th century builders.

men allot so much ground about their houses for pleasure of gardens and orchards' wrote Fynes Morrison in 1617, by which time the achievements of the previous century were plain to see. More peaceful times under the Tudors had obviated the need for houses to be strongholds and made it feasible for them to be turned into comfortable homes instead. Surrounding grounds were treated as additional living space, divided into separate compartments laid out in different ways and linked by terraced or hedged paths. The Tudor sovereigns were responsible for setting an example in the establishment of palace gardens, as at Hampton Court and Nonsuch; on a smaller scale and according to means, their subjects followed suit. Francis Bacon considered a house to be incomplete without a well-ordered garden to set if off, and implied that of the two, the second was the greater achievement. Certainly when houses were being improved or rebuilt during the 16th century, equal attention was given to the layout of the grounds and to the introduction of currently popular features – a raised terrace or mound whence the whole garden might be viewed: a knot garden where hedges of lavender, box or hyssop enclosed small plots filled with coloured pebbles or earth: an orchard: and sheltered paths leading from one area to another. Scents as well as colour were important, so there were flower beds also, filled with traditional flowers – roses, pinks, jasmine and violets, and new imported plants and shrubs – tulips, auriculae, lilac and syringa.

Inevitably the basic plan of Tudor gardens has since been overlaid or destroyed according to later fashions, and although here and there, whether by chance or design, 16th century features have been reproduced, it is rarely possible to claim that a garden has remained unchanged until today. Thornbury Castle, perhaps because it was left unfinished and untouched for

Thornbury Castle: the Courtyard, site of the Privy Garden.

Chipping Campden: a Summer House, a remaining feature of Campden House.

so long, has retained some of its original layout, with an orchard once 'thick sett with trees of diverse kinds of fruit', clipped hedges and an open courtyard overlooked by the windows of the State apartments. The courtyard was probably the site of the Privy Garden, ornamented by a knot garden of elaborate heraldic design, for the making of which John Wynde, gardener, was paid 3 shillings and 4 pence by the Duke of Buckingham, owner and builder of Thornbury. At Sudeley, where Sir Giles Brydges improved the house and gardens in anticipation of entertaining the Queen during her visits to Gloucestershire, there is a yew hedge clipped and shaped like a gallery with alcoves at intervals, affording sheltered openings. This is reminiscent of the topiary work that might well have been introduced into the garden in the late 16th century. The terraces at Owlpen Manor and Upper Slaughter Manor, overlooking enclosed areas of gardens are also reminders of Tudor features; and the mound at Stanway, introduced in the 18th century, would not have looked out of place adjoining the house when this was built c.1580. Of fountains and other water effects such as were introduced at Wilton House during the 16th century, there are no remains or records in Gloucestershire; nor do contemporary writings refer to banqueting houses, popular in the late 16th century, though these may have been built in the grounds of larger houses and have since disappeared. One exception to this is at Chipping Campden where the only remaining features of the mansion built by Sir Baptist Hicks in 1613 are two summer houses situated at each end of the terrace that once fronted the house.

There was in Tudor Gloucestershire a considerable number of wealthy families able to indulge their taste for entertainment, whose presence created a steady demand for groups of actors and musicians with a capacity for responding spontaneously to the needs of the moment, be this a religious festival, the visit of some important personage or a family occasion. Until his disgrace and execution in 1521, the Duke of Buckingham at Thornbury, in keeping with his royal descent and seigneurial ambitions, enjoyed the most magnificent life style in the county, followed closely by the Berkeleys, and the Brydges of Sudeley, while lesser families emulated their superiors when and as they could afford. The wealthiest had their own troupes of players who resided with them and often accompanied them on journeys and visits, but who were free and indeed expected to maintain themselves elsewhere when not needed by their patrons. This is why there are references in the Gloucester Borough Records to payments made to the players of Lord Ambrose Dudley, Master Kyngestone, the Countess of Suffolk, also of 'the Queen's Majestie', since during the latter's visits to Gloucester she graciously allowed her court entertainers to perform for the benefit of the citizens. Although the plays and musical entertainments staged at Thornbury, Berkeley and other mansions were performed primarily for the benefit of the owners and their families, local gentry and officials might be invited along with tenants, estate employees and neighbouring villagers. Christmas, Easter and Whitsun were favoured times for elaborately staged and costumed pieces; also family occasions such as a christening, a marriage or a coming of age would be similarly celebrated and the whole neighbourhood be made to feel a party to what was happening. If resident players were not available, then local talent might be conscripted to entertain at the great house – mummers, fiddlers, Morris dancers and jugglers – so that the presentation and enjoyment of diversions was always a reciprocal affair between a wealthy household and people living in its vicinity.

The 'middling' folk who bridged the gap between the wealthy and poor were most numerous in the towns, though they had their equivalent in the countryside among the lesser gentry and successful yeoman farmers. It was typical of members of this class as a whole to be ambitious and to model their social life as far as possible on that of their superiors, even if opportunities to do so were limited. Within the confines of a town there were no wide open spaces for hunting and coursing, but there was room for archery butts and bowling greens, and many individuals had dogs and horses and might go riding in the country sometimes. More usually the

Winchcombe: the galleried courtyard of the George Inn.

townsmen enjoyed 'spectator' sports like bull-baiting, cock-fighting and bouts of wrestling, all of which were rendered the more exciting as they afforded opportunities for gambling on the outcome – another popular and widespread diversion in the 16th century. People in the towns were also able to take advantage of the entertainment provided by civic officials who processed to church each Sunday, and on the occasions of the election of a Mayor, the holding of a Council meeting, or the patronal day of a parish church. Still, in the 16th century the Craft guilds were fulfilling social as well as economic functions, putting on pageants and plays at religious festivals such as Christmas and Easter. Guild members too proceeded to their meetings, courts and chapels in ceremonial guise. The rules of the Tanners' Company in Gloucester enjoined that the Master should always be dressed in fine clothes, and that 'Every member is to assemble in best apparel with badge on shoulder on the eve of St. John and of St. Peter'. And while the Guild processions provided entertainment for the townsfolk in general, the Guild feasts were an exclusive diversion for members alone, tables being sumptuously laid with gold and silver plate, lavish amounts of food and drink elaborately served, and musicians helping to while away the time between courses.

The Market Square at Lechlade.

As well as the entertainment derived from official civic occasions, (and in some places background music regularly provided by the waits) town dwellers could rely on the services of itinerant players who travelled the countryside taking in as many places as had potential audiences. The towns and larger villages provided not only these but suitable places for performances as well, either galleried courtyards like that of the New Inn at Gloucester and the George at Winchcombe, or market places as at Tetbury, Lechlade and Cirencester, where a platform could be erected or a wide area cleared, still leaving room for spectators to view the proceedings. Some of the players, as we have noticed, were employees of patrons, filling in time between commissioned engagements; some belonged to companies entirely dependent for a living on their ability to command attention and win applause from casual audiences; still others might be amateurs, hopeful of earning extra pence by putting on an extempore entertainment of one sort or another, like those at Cheltenham:

> William Dobbins sounded his drumme up and downe the towne in the tyme of markett accompanied with Richard Clerke and divers other younge fellowes being artificers and laborers, the said Richard Clerke following the said Dobbins sounding his drumme with a truncheon or short staffe in his hand in the maner of a lyutenant or marshall man . . .

caused proclamacion to be made in divers places of the said towne, publiquely proclayming that whosoever would have a play should come to the signe of the Crowne such an howre where they intended to play.

Fairs and markets which were regular features of urban life had an unfailing attraction for entertainers and those wishing to be entertained. These were ideal times for players to resort to the towns where they would be joined by jugglers, tumblers, minstrels and men with performing animals, sure of capturing the attention of a crowd bent on enjoyment. But even without diversions, such occasions were a satisfying entertainment in themselves for merchants and craftsmen whose livelihood was dependent on buying and selling, and whose lives were dominated by ambitions such as making profitable business deals and acquiring material goods to enhance their homes and their own appearance and thus to reflect their success in the eyes of the world. In the 16th century, as it is today, town life promised a more action-packed and colourful existence than life in the country could possibly do. The crowded streets, innumerable shops and stalls, background noise and brisk tempo of life accorded with the aspirations of any who were bitten with the restlessness of the age and had the desire and ability to break out of a traditional, trammelling routine. For these, just to be part of an urban community was an entertainment in itself.

By comparison dwellers in the country were still tied to a demanding and monotonous routine that discouraged enterprise and limited hours of leisure. The pattern of their days was dictated by natural circumstances such as the weather and condition of the land, and their holiday calendar determined by landmarks in the farming year, i.e. the intervals between the completion of one season of labour and the beginning of another, when one day or more would be given up to eating, drinking, revelling and various sports with prizes to be competed for. Harvest time was perhaps the most important of these feasts since this marked the completion of the agricultural year when work slacked off for a while and most people had more money to spend than usual.

This age-old routine of farming life was so firmly established that other events came to be dovetailed with it – the markets and fairs, for instance – and especially the statute fairs which marked the beginning and end of a year of employment for labourers and domestic servants. Parish wakes, too, were arranged to fit in with farming activities. These were normally held on or near the feast day of the saint to whom the parish church was dedicated, but as well there would be others during the late spring and early autumn when farm workers had most leisure. The wakes lasted for several days and were occasions for general roistering in which dancing, minstrelsie, rough games and excessive drinking played a large part. Even the parish priest might get carried away in the excitement. At Weston sub

Edge in 1574, 'Michael Hyndmer, Rector, answereth that in a Christmas hollydaye he went a masking and that there was ann egge brok'; and at Mitcheldean in 1602, '13 people were prosecuted for piping and dancing and John Sylmott, Rector, led the dance.' Dancing appears to have had more liberating influence even than drink and to have been imbued with all kinds of suggestiveness, which explains why – as Puritan ideas took a firmer hold towards the end of the century – any occasions for it, like the parish wakes, began to be frowned upon. The close association between the church and parochial pleasures is reflected in the string course at Cirencester where a line of stone figures, carrying various musical instruments, represents the Whitsun wake procession.

Until the Reformation, other welcome breaks in the farming year had been the obligatory observance of major church festivals, Christmas, Easter and Whitsun, and numerous Saints' days. The abolition of some of these 'superstitious practices' at the time of the Reformation affected country folk to a greater extent than town dwellers since the former had fewer alternative diversions; so any that did remain were celebrated the more wholeheartedly. It was on these occasions that local talent came into action – teams of bellringers, Morris dancers and Maypole dancers, waits, wassailers and amateur actors – performing music, dances and plays that were traditional to the locality, never recorded but handed down orally from one generation to another. Most of these had a moral or religious element though some were rooted in pagan rites and others in legends such as those of St. George and Robin Hood. However, any serious intent there may have been originally in the festivities was soon outweighed by a single-minded pursuit of pleasure, as Hugh Latimer discovered in 1549 when on arriving at a place where he had announced his intention of preaching 'because it was holy day', he found the church door locked and no one to greet him. After a wait of half an hour or so the key was found, but one of the parishioners came to him and said, 'Sir, this a busy day with us, we cannot hear you, it is Robin Hood's day. The parish are gone abroad to gather for Robin Hood'. The aggrieved Bishop took this less light-heartedly than his potential congregation. 'It is a weeping matter . . . to prefer Robin Hood before the ministration of God's word'.

A great number of country towns and villages in Gloucestershire could lay claim to their own particular mumming play, wassail song, Maypole or Morris dances, some of which are still performed today. Mumming was primarily associated with Christmas, and although versions of the play varied from place to place, the characters were stock ones and usually included Father Christmas, St. George and the Doctor. Occasionally the mumming play was performed at other times of the year as at Snowshill where it took place on the feast of St. Barnabas, patron saint of the parish church. Wassailing too was a Christmas activity, with songs reminding people of the need for seasonal generosity and the circulation of a wassail bowl to hold largesse, essential parts of the proceedings. Some places in the south of the county – Randwick, Woodchester, Avening – were known for their wassailing songs, and Minchinhampton had a 'King of the Wassailers' who kept the bowl throughout the year. The wassail bowl was usually elaborately decorated, as was also the Maypole which was brought out for the May Day celebrations; both demonstrated the skill of the villagers to use the greenery and flowers of the countryside to good effect. Dances were a feature of the May Day festivities and special ones were associated with Bledington, Chipping Campden, Nailsworth and Spelsbury. Although most villages had their own Morris sides, a small group of villages in the North Cotswolds – Bledington, Longborough and Oddington, thanks to the researches and recording of Cecil Sharp early in this century, have become particularly well-known for their dances, some of which may well date back to the 16th century.

While contrasting the lot of town and country dwellers, somewhat to the disadvantage of the latter, it must be remembered that in the field or in the house they were working in a relaxed atmosphere that allowed for singing, the exchange of gossip and the telling of stories; and although their week was a six-day one, Sunday was always a day of leisure when obligatory church attendance was followed by indulgence in outdoor activities and general conviviality at the village inn. In the interest of national military strength, men were encouraged to practise archery and indulge in running, leaping, football and other sports that would promote physical fitness; in addition any pleasurable activities were allowed, provided that they did not become too violent (football was notoriously rough and dangerous to person and property) or were carried on during the time of divine service. At the inn, games of cards, dicing and gambling on a small scale amused the older and less athletic.

As in the case of the occasional parish wakes, regular Sunday amusements roused the disapproval of the Puritans during the closing years of the century. This was partly because they held that any secular activity constituted a breach of the Sabbath which they believed should be devoted strictly to religious purposes: and partly because they were convinced any form of relaxation that might lead to extremes, was better avoided altogether. And in spite of a general desire to enjoy Sundays in traditional fashion, there were enough Puritanically inclined people in Gloucestershire to fulminate against the Sabbath breakers, and county members supported measures in Parliament to make the Elizabethan Church Settlement even more strongly Protestant than it was. A certain Anthony Bridgeman (not a member of Parliament) managed to gain access to the Palace in 1589, with a petition in hand entitled 'A New Year's Gift' in which he requested that the Queen should introduce some social and religious reforms, including 'a

COTSWOLD GAMES.

The Cotswold Games on Dover's Hill at Chipping Campden.

restraint of the profaning of the Saboth day, especially with minstrelsie, baiting of bears and other beasts'. A Master of Requests took the petition and quietly suppressed it, as did Walsingham when he was presented with another copy of it a little while later.

Such determined opposition to Sunday sports and indeed any light-hearted pleasures might well have had the effect of suppressing them altogether (as happened during the Commonwealth period) but Elizabeth and her successor James I both gave an official blessing to them and thus ranked themselves with the majority of their subjects. That we know the form they took and that they were preserved for posterity was largely due to Robert Dover, a Warwickshire lawyer, who early in the 17th century, initiated and organised the early Cotswold Games at Chipping Campden: and to his friend Endymion Porter, a Gloucestershire gentleman of Aston sub Edge, who interested James I in the venture, gained his approval for it, and even begged some of the King's cast-off clothes for Dover to wear while officiating as Master of Ceremonies. In a book 'Annalia Dubrensia' published in 1617 to celebrate the Games, there is a frontispiece which pictures rustics playing at cudgels, wrestling, jumping, tossing the hammer, leap-frogging and standing on their hands, while wealthier men and women are shown dancing, coursing and hunting.

The enthusiasm that people brought to their pleasures in the 16th century was typical of the age. Greater stability and prosperity enabled men of all classes to have and to enjoy leisure time, while increasing secularism encouraged them to do this with clear consciences and wholehearted abandon. Growing independence, confidence and gaiety were reflected in contemporary music, dancing and plays, while a spirit of competition heightened the interest of those who watched or took part in sporting activities. The wealthy might relax in the privacy of their homes or enjoy ranging the countryside in pursuit of furred or feathered prey, whereas the humbler sort got together in the alehouse or on the village green; but at the same time no class barriers divided people in their delight at plays, pageants and processions. Those who watched plays, whether from privileged seats or from the pit, equally well appreciated the performances of their theatrical counterparts – the country gentlemen, the singers and dancers, the clowns, 'the hard handed men that work', and rustic shepherds and shepherdesses. They shared an enjoyment of music too whether performed adeptly on the virginals, scraped out by a village fiddler, or blared forth in the fanfare of trumpets that accompanied the arrival, presence and departure of important personages, or heralded the making of an important announcement. (Trumpets as well as drums and pipes were among the instruments played by the town waits, who were expected to perform on all public occasions). And dancing, whether a graceful measure, a brisk jig or a country romp, brought an uninhibited lightness of heart to rich and poor alike. Whether it was realised or not, Renaissance influences were spreading in England; and foreigners who commented on the capacity of the English to enjoy themselves, were also drawing attention to the freedom, opportunities and means that enabled them to do so.

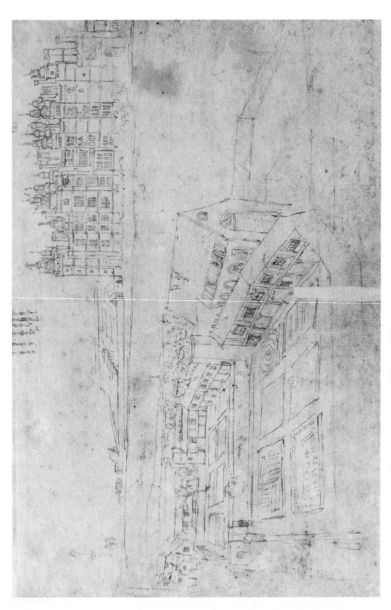

The Palace of Richmond at Sheen: a residence of Henry VII.

9

Lasting Memorials . . .

'The golden days and all the world amended.'

Commenting on the desirability or otherwise of change, Francis Bacon wrote: 'Time itself innovateth greatly but quietly', and the history of Gloucestershire in the 16th century bears this out. During this transition period there was no sharp break between the world of the Middle Ages and a modern one like enough to the present day to be intelligible, but rather a dovetailing and an over-lapping, so that as early as the start of the century there were signs of preparedness for change and even of change itself, while at the close of it there were still pockets of mediaevalism surviving.

During the Middle Ages life had been dominated by the twin forces of feudalism and the Church, the visible signs of which were castles and fortified manor houses on the one hand, abbeys and parish churches on the other. In Gloucestershire for lack of use, some castles had disappeared by the end of the 15th century – Miserden, Brimpsfield and St. Briavels for instance. Only Berkeley and Beverstone, both owned by the Berkeley family, and Sudeley, held as a royal stronghold by the Botelers until the 16th century, retained their embattled appearance, but even here the addition of domestic buildings had begun to blur their former grim outlines. This makes it all the more surprising that Thornbury Castle, the one large new residence begun in the early 16th century should have been planned primarily as a fortress, just when the fashion (as set by the Tudor monarchs) was veering towards stylish comfort rather than greater security. We cannot tell whether Thornbury, had it been completed, would have resembled Henry VII's palace-castle of Richmond at Sheen rather than Henry VIII's royal residence at Hampton Court, since its impressive entrance with a turreted gatehouse and battlemented walls are at odds with the high oriel windows and elaborately decorative chimneys of the state apartments at the rear. Berkeley and Sudeley, although adapted during the course of the century to receive Tudor monarchs making progresses round

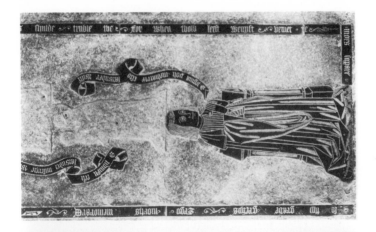

Brasses at Northleach. (a) *William Midwinter* (b) *Thomas Busshe* (c) *William Lander, a priest.*

The tomb of John and Edmund Tame at Fairford.

the county, neverthless remained as reminders of their feudal significance – strongholds held by tenants-in-chief owing military service to the king. ₤

Of the great monastic buildings, most were virtually destroyed at the dissolution. In some cases, even the foundations disappeared, but at Hailes and Lantony at Gloucester, skeletal walls and arches remained and can still be seen. Of the abbey churches, Cirencester, Deerhurst and Winchcombe which had also been used for parish services, were saved for this purpose. Tewkesbury should have been razed to the ground along with the monks' domestic quarters, but the purchase of the church by the townsfolk seems to have halted the wholesale destruction, for the abbey gate-house, barn and guest house were also left. The abbey churches of St. Augustine at Bristol and St. Peter at Gloucester survived to become the cathedrals of the new dioceses created by Henry VIII in 1541–42. All these churches thus linked Gloucestershire's Catholic past with its Protestant future in the late 16th century.

Churches which were at the heart of popular religion became promotion centres for reform under Edward VI and Elizabeth. Priests were supposed to preach the new doctrines from the pulpit, while the interiors of the churches were adapted to Protestant services. The abolition of prayers for

John Cooke: Sheriff and Mayor of Gloucester, and his wife Joan.

the dead, intercession to the saints and altar lights ended the mediaeval practice of bequests being made for such purposes; instead more material and lasting memorials than special masses and flickering candles were devised for those who died. Brasses, so much favoured by the wool merchants in the 15th century, continued to mark their resting places in the churches up to the end of the 16th century. The particularly splendid collection at Northleach was enriched by the addition of memorials to prominent local merchants: William Midwinter and his wife (dated 1501) both pictured with their feet resting on sheep: and Thomas Busshe and his wife (dated 1526) with sheep and a woolpack at their feet. Cirencester too had a 16th century brass to a woolmerchant Philip Marner (1587): Minchinhampton, to a clothier named William Halyday (1519): and Fairford church, which in itself is a monument to their successful careers, has two brasses fixed to slabs of Purbeck marble, one commemorating John Tame (1500) and the other his son Sir Edmund (1534) who between them with money gained from trading in wool and cloth, were responsible for rebuilding the nave, chancel and tower in the early years of the century. And lest it might seem that brasses were the monopoly of wool merchants, it should be mentioned that priests were similarly commemorated at Blockley and Northleach: several generations of the landowning Stephens family at Eastington: civic dignatories like John Cooke, Sheriff and Mayor of Gloucester (1544), who with his wife Joan was buried in St. Mary le Crypt church and together remembered for 'their bountye and beneficence'; and most unusual of all, a woman who died in childbirth, Anne Savage at Wormington, shown with her baby lying in an Elizabethan four poster bed complete with curtains and valances.

As the century progressed, Renaissance ideas took root and flourished. Rich men began to follow the example of nobles and monarchs, planning elaborate tombs for themselves and their families: becoming more specific in their demand for designs seen and admired elsewhere, and effigies 'cutt, graven and colored to the life'; since, according to current thinking which exalted the dignity of man as an individual and set great store by his achievements, it seemed important that the subject of the memorial should be recognised from his effigy and remembered as he had been in his prime. Materials – alabaster, stone, paint and gilt – were expensive, even more so than the workmanship bestowed on them; but this was a competitive age, and since it was expedient in life to dress, eat and live as sumptuously as means allowed, so after death, tombs must measure up to the same standards:

> Sepulchres should be made according to the qualitie and degree of the person deceased, that by the tombe every one might be discerned of what ranke hee was living; for monuments answerable to men's birth, states and places, have alwayes beene allowed.*

The wealthy who lived near London were able to obtain the finest materials and employ the best craftsmen (Italian early in the 16th century, Flemish later) to produce memorials they considered worthy of their families. However, books of patterns and emblems, increasingly available as the century went on, provided a range of designs which skilled local workers were able to reproduce successfully. A satisfied client or a widely commended piece of work would serve to secure further commissions, so that recognisable styles and mannerisms can be found in some localities. Most of the makers of tombs remained anonymous, but Samuel Baldwin of Stroud employed initially by Lady Berkeley, became known for his work in Gloucestershire and Worcestershire, exhibiting such skill and acquaintance with fashionable contemporary styles that Mrs. Esdaile (in *English Church Monuments*) considers he may well have spent some time training under a first-rate London master after an apprenticeship in Bristol.

* Weaver: *Funerall Monuments*

The marble tomb of Sir William Leigh and his wife at Longborough.

Quite as much as their houses, the monuments of 16th century families reflect the satisfaction of socially successful men as well as contemporary values and taste. The full length effigies on table tombs showed figures clad in the height of fashion, often reclining with their hands under their heads:

> They are no longer fashioned with their eyes fixed upon the stars,
> But as their minds were wholly bent upon the world
> The selfsame way they seem to turn their faces*

Sons and daughters who survived, and even babes who did not, were depicted along the sides or front of the tomb, and any available space filled with emblems – shells, leaves, heraldic devices. The most elaborate designs included a canopy supported by decorative pillars. The tomb of Humfry Bridges (d. 1598) and his family at Cirencester, the work of Samuel Baldwin mentioned above, is in local stone, painted and canopied, with kneeling figures of two sons at the head and feet of their parents and nine other children pictured between carved columns on the panel below. At Almondsbury, the tomb of Edward Veele (d. 1577) reflects to an even greater extent contemporary Renaissance influence, with fluted columns supporting a canopy decorated with blazonry. The monument to John Trye (d. 1591) and his son at Hardwicke, also extremely ornate and rich in heraldry, is rather unusual in that the father is portrayed not in contemporary costume but in armour. Another armoured figure (early 17th

* Webster: *The Duchess of Malfi.*

Cirencester: the tomb of Humfry Bridges, work of Samuel Baldwin.

century) is that of Sir William Leigh at Longborough, who lies with his wife and three children, all sculpted in white marble, while contrasting black marble has been used for the pillared canopy that shelters them. The Throckmorton tomb at Tortworth (1568) is striking in every respect, fashioned in alabaster with a magnificent canopy and backed by a panel filled with devices and emblems; and equally outstanding is another example of the work of Samuel Baldwin, the monument to Thomas Stephens at Stroud, a kneeling effigy of painted and gilded alabaster whose ornateness closely resembles memorials in London churches and confirms the view that Baldwin was acquainted with work being done in the capital.

The marked lack of church building during the 16th century was due in part to the religious changes which cast doubts about the future even among those who were in favour of them. There is no doubt also, that men's thoughts and money were increasingly being directed towards worldly objectives. Nevertheless, here and there, additions and innovations were

A Column in the Nave at Cirencester with the distinguishing shield of a benefactor.

made. Eastington acquired a new aisle, financed by the Duke of
Buckingham before his downfall in 1521: the north aisle of Aldsworth was
rebuilt and enriched with much fine carving: a tower, fashioned out of
materials from Hailes Abbey was added to Toddington church. Between
1516 and 1530 wealthy merchants in Cirencester subscribed funds for
rebuilding the nave of their church in contemporary Perpendicular style, the
arms or marks of the contributors being recorded in shields on each side of
the piers supporting the immensely high roof. Two churches were virtually
rebuilt, one at Cold Ashton paid for by its rector Thomas Key: the other at
Fairford, perhaps the most notable achievement of the century. Completed
within the life span of father and son, John and Edmund Tame between
1490 and 1534, and therefore structurally integrated and homogeneous in
style, it survived iconoclastic zeal under Edward VI and retained all its
original features, including the richly carved stalls and screens in the choir
and the huge perpendicular windows of the nave filled with fine glass
specially made for them, the work of Bernard Flower, Henry VII's Master
Glass Painter.

However, although there were only a few significant changes in
buildings, a large number of town and village churches acquired new plate –
chalices, patens, bowls, alms-dishes and candlesticks – mostly dated in the
early years of Elizabeth's reign. Some were bought out of parish funds,

Cirencester: The Boleyn Cup.

others donated by benefactors. Many individual items in silver and gilt are unique but the most interesting set of church plate is considered to be that belonging to Cirencester, which includes pairs of beautifully designed chalices and flagons and the gilt Boleyn cup dated 1535 and bearing the badge of the Boleyn family. Items of plate with intrinsic and rarity value nowadays were expensive even in the 16th century, and that people were ready to donate these and other gifts indicated the extent to which the church and its services still played a part in their lives even though perhaps less obviously and obtrusively than in earlier times. This very real respect and affection is reflected in the message accompanying a donation to Lechlade church in 1558, by John Organ of London:

> For the love and zeale that he doth beare unto the Towne and Parysshe of Leachlade, and for that he was there borne, he hathe given a herse clothe of Silke and goulde, with Fringe of silk round it.

Thomas Poulton of Tewkesbury likewise sought to benefit both the church and parishioners by bequeathing in his will to the town of Cheltenham:

Winchcombe: Borough Seals.

One Booke of Acts and Monuments with a Chaine of Yron to be placed in Churche on a deske where every man that will, maye come and take Profitte thereby.

As we have seen, there was a marked expansion of trade both domestic and foreign during the course of the 16th century paralleled by a growing amount of business in the towns, to meet the demands of which urban facilities were augmented and the machinery of town government became more elaborate and formalised. By the end of the century most towns had a building where urban officials and townspeople met to deal with matters of common concern, for example the church porch at Cirencester, the new Town Hall at Tewkesbury, the Court House at Stow on the Wold; and in places where there were regular markets, buildings or special locations were set aside for the examination, pricing and sale of goods, and for the holding of courts to enforce special market regulations. Towns that had elected officials and established constitutions, in order to surround their customary procedures with an aura of antiquity, recorded them in detail, as did also the craft guilds. There is a close similarity between all these records; the civic officials in most places had much the same work to do and problems to contend with, likewise the Masters and Wardens of the guilds, but it was important that each town and the various craftsmen should be recognised and acknowledged as individual cases. The Gloucester Borough Records well illustrate this point.

Markets and fairs, features that helped to distinguish and enhance town life during the Middle Ages, became even more significant during the 16th century. Their importance was underlined in that towns with market rights included in their charters had the latter confirmed regularly at the start of each new reign, while those without such privileges tried to acquire them. The people of Winchcombe were successful in this, and the wording of the charter granted by Elizabeth in 1585 reveals what they hoped to gain from it:

> As well as for the repaire as the improvement, relief and enhancement of the said towne . . . we would vouchsafe to grant one faire in every yeare and one market in every weeke . . .

At the same time, to those that had, more was given. Gloucester, increasing steadily in the size of its population and business, and already recognised as a county town since 1483, was granted recognition as a port, and a monopolistic control of traffic up and down the Severn by an additional charter in 1580:

> Whereas no wharf or landing for shipping foreign goods is assigned at Gloucester or above it on the Severn . . . in consideration of the great population of Gloucester and for the convenience of Gloucester, Worcester and Shrewsbury . . . all creeks are to be regarded as a port and the common quay of Gloucester, King's Quay, a lawful and proper place for loading and unloading.

Not all towns advanced during the 16th century. Some that were too closely bound to serving neighbouring estates (e.g. Berkeley) or exclusively identified with the wool trade (e.g. Northleach, Chipping Campden) declined and lost their importance; but those near to road and river routes, and capable also of adjusting to new circumstances, enhanced their strength and status. Stow on the Wold at the confluence of five cross-country roads, and Newnham on Severn at the convergence of Forest of Dean routes on a crossing of the river, both provided market facilities for traders and benefited from their presence and passage. Cirencester exploited its proximity to the developing cloth trade in the Stroud area, and Lechlade to the huge demand from London for agricultural products that could be collected from the Cotswold area and despatched via the Thames to the capital. Bristol, with the greatest advantages in the country in view of its position facing the newly developing trade routes to southern Europe and America, made the most of its wide hinterland as a source of goods for export and a distribution area for imports. Soon the bulk of its trade put it well ahead of all other ports in the west, while the wealth and dignity of its populace, the scale of its buildings and its status as a cathedral city inspired comparison with London.

The towns that were flourishing at the end of the 16th century remained as focal points in their locality for the next two centuries. Quite as much as the disappearance of castles, their existence and survival marks the end of feudalism and the arrival of a new age wherein economic forces and opportunities of gain counted for more than security and the fulfilment of obligations between master and dependent. In the towns to a greater degree than anywhere else careers were open to talent and there was social mobility as opposed to a class structure predetermined by birth or family circumstances. This is reflected in the success of craftsmen and merchants who rose to civic dignities, built houses worthy of their status, left wills which list furniture, hangings, carpets, collections of plate and fine clothes, including, in the case of Sir Thomas Bell of Gloucester, 'my velvet gowne and my velvet Coate, a damaske gowne furred with black conye, a damaske gowne faced with black velvet, a doublet of Crymsyn satten and a satten gowne furryd with foynes, a coat of branchid damaske garded with velvet and a tawny damaske dublet with skyrte'. They also left bequests to their towns, generous sums of money for schools, almshouses, hospitals, the upkeep of roads and bridges. Personal pride was herein intermingled with public conscience and it would be hard to draw a dividing line between the two.

In places like Gloucester and Cirencester that continued to develop, 16th century buildings have been altered or completely rebuilt, and only isolated features remain – Tudor doorways, Renaissance mouldings and emblems and mullion windows. In smaller places that did not enjoy a later heyday there are more easily discernible traces of what Hoskins called 'the great rebuilding'. Winchcombe has its Chandos almshouses, the George Hotel and the Old Corner Cupboard Inn: Chipping Campden some town houses fronting the High Street, and the almshouses built by Sir Baptist Hicks soon after the end of the 16th century: Tewkesbury the Old Fleece Inn and a number of half-timbered buildings over hanging its main street. From the mediaeval huddle of cottages, workshops and alehouses the Tudor period had produced recognisable towns with wider, straighter streets, more permanent dwellings, official buildings and inns that impressed travellers by their cleanliness and hospitality. According to Harrison: 'Our inns are very well furnished . . . the linen used at the tables is commonly washed daily . . . and each comer is sure to lie in clean sheets wherein no man has been lodged since they came from the laundress.'* Tables were laid with plate and there was a considerable choice of food and wines; and music might be provided at meals by the town waits – not necessarily a recommendation perhaps.

In the countryside, one of the most marked and lasting changes visible by the end of the 16th century was the increased amount of traffic on the roads, which incidentally served to emphasise how much the roads themselves

---

* Harrison: *The Description of England.*

The convergence of routes at Stow on the Wold.

needed to be improved. Grassy tracks, undefined and unsignposted, with a tendency to disappear under seas of mud in winter and clouds of dust in summer, had served local farmers and transient traders during the Middle Ages, but were neither adequate nor durable enough for the traffic occasioned by increased local output and a general expansion of trade. So along with their many other activities Justices of the Peace were saddled with responsibility for the roads, to ensure that holes and ruts were filled in, fallen trees removed, ditches cleared and bridges made safe to cross. The necessary maintenance work was supposed to be carried out by local unpaid labour, but it proved difficult to induce men to fulfil their obligations in this respect, and in fact any work done or materials used were frequently paid

Winchcombe: the Old Corner Cupboard Inn built in the 16th century.

Entertainments at an Inn (a) The Waits (b) Dinner (c) A quiet smoke.

for by the Justice himself. The announcement of a Royal progress could work wonders in producing a full turn-out of workers and visible results; otherwise the state of the roads remained variable and uncertain, except near towns where civic pride and money from benefactors maintained approaches in reasonably good repair. However, in spite of the hazards, road travel and transport were indispensable, and it is significant that during the course of Elizabeth's reign the cartographer John Norden introduced the practice of marking roads in his maps which also had marginal numbers to enable users to find any places they wanted.

The trains of pack-horses, loaded waggons and herds of sheep and cattle passing to and from local markets, and through the county either to ports on the Severn or towards the Midlands and London, churned up the roads in Gloucestershire considerably more quickly than they could be repaired. So it was no wonder that during the 16th century navigable rivers were brought into use as a cheap and reliable means of moving heavy goods such as corn, coal and timber, iron and salt; and that attempts were begun to improve the flow of water and to keep channels safe and clear for shipping, even in the face of opposition from owners of mills and makers of weirs

Bristol in the 16th Century.

who had exploited the rivers for their own purposes for many years and were naturally reluctant to give up what they considered to be their rights. Of all places in the county Bristol gained most from the development of river traffic. Situated at the confluence of the Avon and the Severn and not far from where the Wye joins the latter, it was able to monopolise the export trade from the Welsh border counties, the Midlands and Gloucestershire: and to canalise imports from Europe, Africa and America through its own docks and warehouses via river to places inland. Gloucester benefited from its position at the head of the Severn estuary, and Tewkesbury from being sited at the junction of the Warwickshire Avon with the Severn. Lesser ports like Lydney and Newnham offered facilities for loading and unloading the craft that plied along the Severn, linking river traffic with sea-going vessels at Bristol. Meanwhile, at the head of navigation on the Thames, Lechlade was gaining from the use of its quays by the barges that carried agricultural products from Gloucestershire to London. By the end of the 16th century river traffic was established as an important factor in the economic life of the county and of England as a whole. Therefore it was natural that John Leland, collecting material for his *Itinerary*, should announce his intention of visiting 'every haven, creek or pier, river or confluence of rivers' during his survey of England: and that Christopher Saxton, one of our earliest map-makers, should have marked very emphatically the river systems and estuaries in each county that he delineated.

Finally, among the lasting features of the 16th century must be mentioned the rise of the gentry, socially and politically of considerable significance in Gloucestershire since it was from their ranks that the county drew its official administrators when these were needed. As landowners they led the way in improving farm practices: by means of their wealth they were able to help the needy, provide employment for workers and extend patronage to craftsmen: and by virtue of their own knowledge and enthusiasm, they promoted the ideas and ideals of the Renaissance which dominated the culture of the 16th century. The outward signs of their arrival were the houses they built, designed as showpieces of their success as well as a setting for the comfortable and civilised life they wanted for themselves and their families. 'The country houses and their enlightened and often powerful occupants were one of the main growing points of English society in its struggle to emerge from the Middle Ages in the 16th century'. Old established families as well as newcomers to the scene were alike in trying to create a favourable image of themselves by means of building projects, and although some of their houses, like surrounding gardens, have entirely disappeared, and almost all have been altered or added to subsequently, neverthless enough features remain to give us an idea of the owners' tastes and values.

Horton Court: the Ambulatory, modelled on an Italian loggia.

The outlook of those who were both the products and the shapers of their times was determined by upbringing and experience. As contemporary conventions and literature (e.g. Sir Thomas Elyot; *The Governour*) laid down guide lines for the training of young men destined for public life in one capacity or another, and as conformity with social usage was considered essential, the sons of successful together with those of still aspiring families, went through much the same training – a public school, University or Inns of Court, and foreign travel. Their years in England brought them into contact with others of their own generation and outlook, and frequently established links that were to prove valuable later on. Those who went abroad and visited France and Italy experienced at first hand the artistic and literary Renaissance there and brought home with them a knowledge and appreciation of classical architecture and learing that was to have a lasting effect on them and the country as a whole. The case of William Knight, Prothonotary of the Holy See and later Bishop of Bath and Wells, illustrates this point. Knight was educated at Winchester and New College, became a Secretary to Henry VII and a Chaplain to Henry VIII, who sent him abroad on missions to Spain, France, the Low Countries and finally in 1527 to Rome to further the Royal Divorce proceedings against Katherine of

Horton Court: ornate Renaissance doorway.

Bedroom with an Elizabethan bed at Elmore Court.

Aragon. Although a commoner, Knight fared well in royal service and had
a coat of arms devised for and bestowed on him by Henry VIII to
compensate for his humble birth. In 1521 he embarked on the building of
Horton Court where he introduced some of the architectural styles he had
seen abroad. The house had door frames with arabesque decorations, plaster
friezes and ceilings, and Knight's arms carved in stone above the front
entrance and in wood above the chimneypiece in the main living-room.
Detached from the main building was an ambulatory, modelled on an
Italian loggia, its inner wall decorated with plaster medallion heads of
Roman emperors, surely a reflection of scenes that Knight had become
familiar with in Italy.

Those who did not go abroad were not necessarily deprived of knowledge of the latest architectural styles. There were examples of work done by
fashionable craftsmen in London and elsewhere: and books of patterns
produced in the Low Countries and distributed here in the second half of the
century, to become widely used as guides by provincial craftsmen. No well
known contemporary architect builders have been associated with the
houses that were remodelled or newly erected in Gloucestershire during the

An ornate chimney-piece at Chavenage.

16th century, perhaps because none of these were prestigious enough to compare with the projects of wealthy patrons elsewhere such as the Countess of Shrewsbury at Hardwick, Lord Thynne at Longleat or Sir Francis Willoughby at Wollaton. However, Newark Park build c. 1540 by Sir Nicholas Poyntz from the stones of Kingswood Abbey, closely resembled the style of Robert Smythson, and in its early stages, Thornbury certainly promised to be a copy of contemporary royal residences. Elsewhere, both in outline and decorative details, gentry houses conformed with the dictates of fashion, so that just as in respect of church monuments, similarities can be found between them, reflecting the tastes and interests of their owners.

When a new house was planned and the owner was free to choose a site for it, his main consideration was no longer security but that 'the prospect to and fro the place be pleasant, fayre and good to the eye, to beholde the woodes, the waters, the feldes, the vales, the hylles and the playne grounde'. Thus Stowell Park built by Sir Robert Atkynson commanded views across its own grounds and the River Coln to Chedworth woods; Ablington Manor belonging to John Coxwell also overlooked the Coln and its valley down to Bibury. Elmore Court was situated picturesquely within a loop of the River Severn on land that had belonged to the Guise family for centuries; and William Jones, a member of the Haberdashers' Company, chose a site for Naas House near Lydney Harbour whence much of his overseas trade was conducted. If an existing house was retained, its position unchanged, then it was brought into contemporary fashion with larger windows to let in light and air and afford a view of the newly made pleasure garden which now replaced the utilitarian kitchen garden in the area nearest the house, and brought the colours and scents of flower beds and herbs within reach of those indoors. 'I hold it for a most delicate and pleasing thing to have a fair Gallery, great Chamber or other lodging that openeth fully upon the East or West Sun' wrote Sir Hugh Platt in *Floraes Paradise.*

Conscious of the importance of making an immediate and striking impression on their visitors, owners took care that the main entrances to their houses dominated the front facade, so doorways were protected by pillared and often battlemented porches, with carved posts and a decorated entablature, and somewhere a heraldic device, a coat of arms or the owner's initials to establish his achievement and status. Inside, the pursuit of comfort and privacy combined with a love of pageantry and spectacle to produce more rooms for the exclusive use of the family, elaborate panelling for walls and plasterwork for ceilings, and new, magnificent fireplaces commensurate in size and significance with front entrances. Coloured marble, and painted or gilded stone were used for them, with strapwork and carved emblems by way of ornamentation. In the overmantels as well as in ceiling mouldings and in stained glass windows, the arms of the family

Southam: home of the de la Bere family.

were frequently displayed. Those of Daunt and Ollepen appear in a fireplace at Owlpen: of Cassey and Fettiplace in a window at Wightfield: of de la Bere and Huddlestone in an overmantel at Southam: all confirming the gentry status of the owners as well as illustrating the result of the advantageous marriages that had helped to establish them as county landowners.

Inventories and wills are an invaluable guide to the contents of these gentry houses. Although still sparsely furnished as compared with modern homes, they were considerably more fully and more expensively equipped than in earlier centuries. As well as beds, stools and tables, there were chairs, chests, bolsters, cushions, blankets, bed and table linen, pewter and silver and a mass of domestic utensils. Items of clothing and jewellery were valued highly enough to be mentioned individually and emphasised how much money was being spent to achieve a costly appearance. Another indication of means to secure showy luxury was the mention of table carpets, valances and curtains for four poster-beds and wall-hangings. The latter often pictured hunting and other outdoor pursuits, while garden scenes and flowers were especially popular for bedding. And finally there were portraits which, like church ornaments, were designed to catch the likeness of the sitter at the height of his success and thus perpetuate it for posterity. Some, like those of the benefactors of Gloucester, were hung in public places to commenorate their good works. Others were intended for private display in the halls and galleries of the homes of their subjects. As yet, except in court circles, painting was done by local artists and was provincial and even naive in style; but by the end of the 16th century wealthy patrons could command the services of more ape practitioners. The likeness of Thomas Dutton of Sherborne is a competent piece of work which records the confidence of the sitter as well as his stylish beard and single pearl ear-ring.* Sir Giles Brydges and his wife Frances employed the fashionable Hieronimus Custodis to paint their portraits† which are as impressive and as exquisitely detailed (so far as costume is concerned) as any of the court paintings of the time. Clearly the owners of Sudeley were in every way equal to the occasion when the Queen honoured them by her visits.

Against this background of increasingly civilised and gracious living, and maintaining a link between Gloucestershire's past and future were the old families like the Guises, Estcourts and Tracys, outstanding primarily as landowners but important also for their role in local administration. Some names had not survived the Middle Ages – Hungerford, Kingston, Tame, and in the next century that of Clifford too was to disappear – 'The name of Clifford in this County dying with me for want of issue male after 600 years continuance in the same place. Kingdoms and Familys have their periods': as John Clifford reported during the Visitation of the Heralds. But in their place appeared the new men who had established themselves through success in trade, politics or royal favour. The Wynters, originally sea-farers, had acquired estates in the Forest of Dean, and become richer still through exploiting the coal, iron and timber resources there. The Wynter family produced tough, colourful and enterprising personalities, and it is perhaps in keeping that Whitecross, the Elizabethan mansion built by Admiral Sir William Wynter should, during the Civil Wars in the next century, have been defended against the Parliamentary army by the wife of Sir John Wynter, and then burnt by him rather than it should fall into the hands of the enemy. Richard Master, physician to Queen Elizabeth, rewarded with abbey lands at Cirencester, built himself a fashionable house there, set in well laid-out grounds. He was the first of a line that gave service both locally and nationally as Justices, Sheriffs and Members of Parliament. The Duttons, exercising their influence as lords of the manor at Sherborne, dominated the affairs of nearby Northleach. By adding to the nucleus of their estate, they ultimately owned continuous land as far as Cheltenham, where during the 18th century they established a tramroad to carry stone from Leckhampton quarry to Gloucester and bring back coal in return. Having made money in trade, the Atkyns acquired land at Sapperton during

* See page 113.
† See pages 103 and 105.

the 16th century and thereafter produced a succession of skilled lawyers who served as judges in the Royal Courts, as well as the historian of Gloucestershire, Sir Robert Atkyns; while among the immigrants who brought their skills as clothiers to the Stroud area, there was the Paul family, members of which in due course were to make their name not only as successful business men but also as local administrators and phil-anthropists.

Assuredly, the newcomers to Gloucestershire in the 16th century brought new life and enterprise to the area, making their mark at the time as well as starting trends that were to influence the future of the area.

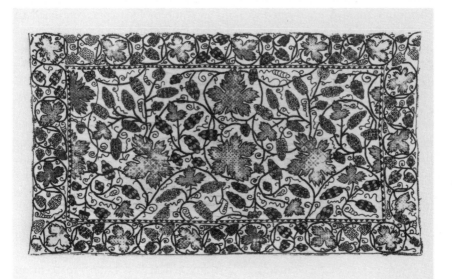

An Elizabethan embroidered pillow.

The End of an Era

Elizabeth I died in 1603 but the spirit of the Tudor Age was to survive for some time after this, so great had been the impetus behind the patriotism, spirit of adventure and loyalty to the monarchy. Fashions in women's costume remained unchanged as long as Anne of Denmark continued to wear out some of the hundreds of dresses left behind by her predecessor; Shakespeare and Ben Jonson continued to write the kind of plays that people had enjoyed ten years before: Sir Baptist Hicks and Thomas Sackville built their new houses at Chipping Campden and Bibury in Tudor style: and there was little to distinguish the Hicks monument at Chipping Campden erected in 1629 from 16th century ones.

However, even before the end of the 16th century, coming events had begun to cast their shadow. Elizabeth's 'solution' of the religious problem had been a compromise and not a permanent settlement and people's acceptance of it lasted only as long as the Queen was alive, indeed in the case of the impatient Puritans not even as long as that: and the government's inability to deal with seditious outbreaks such as the Marprelate Tracts* acted as an incentive to further disaffection.

The Spanish War, at first an exciting and powerful stimulus to all impatient and restless spirits, had lost its initial inspiration, though in fact after the defeat of the Armada almost any action was bound to seem an anticlimax. Moreover, during its course the high cost of the long war became increasingly evident in spite of Elizabeth's attempts to conceal the facts and minimise her demands for money. Common sense as well as political expediency made an end to hostilities desirable long before the Queen's successor James I achieved this. But even the Peace Treaty of 1604 did not satisfy public opinion, for while deploring its expense to the country there were many who had enjoyed the war and felt lost without it. James's unwillingness or inability to subscribe to the legend of Queen and People united in the struggle against the Spanish enemy was one reason for his immediate unpopularity in this country.

Quite unconsciously also, the Queen created a personal problem for her successor who had none of the Tudor charisma, let alone a basic

---

* Marprelate Tracts (1589) published abroad and smuggled into England, they expressed in libellous terms, Puritan disapproval of the episcopacy.

Bibury Court, built by Thomas Sackville in the early 17th century.

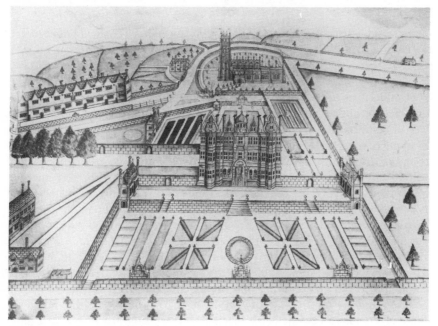

The house and grounds belonging to the Hicks family at Chipping Campden.

The end of an era: the signing of the Peace Treaty between England and Spain (1604).

understanding of the English people which might have enabled James to get his own way without their realising it. Everything about him, and all that he did, failed to come up to expectations so admirably fulfilled by his predecessor. Most importantly, the House of Commons, only narrowly kept under control by the expertise of the Queen and her councillors, very quickly got out of hand when faced with James's impatience and seeming lack of comprehension of English constitutional practice. Existing problems of finance, religion and the issues of war and peace, glossed over or skirted round under Elizabeth, quickly assumed threatening proportions and could neither be shelved nor ignored completely. In spite of his previous success in Scotland, playing off one faction against another and keeping his own power intact meanwhile, James found himself being put in the wrong, defied and quite unable to curb an opposition that was to lead the Civil War during the reign of his son.

Under the Tudors the country experienced peace and mounting prosperity which as well as giving satisfaction also bred self-satisfaction and confidence based on the belief that success was due, in part at any rate, to people's own efforts. The golden haze that surrounded the reign of Elizabeth tended to dazzle her subjects into forgetting just how much they owed to the Tudor sovereigns and their policy. When the new century

*Chipping Campden: the canopied tomb of Sir Baptist
Hicks and his wife.*

ushered in a new dynasty, this seemed the right moment to act on the
strength of convictions that had been engendered by and developed under
the influence of the Renaissance. Even more significantly, circumstances
and events during the 16th century had brought to fruition some of the
potential of the country, and the anxious hesitancy with which people had
faced the future in 1485 had now been replaced by an unprecedented
boldness in the face of challenge and dangers. Even some of the newly-
arrived gentry who owed their rise to the favourable climate created by the
Tudors were prepared to side with those who, on religious or political
grounds, set out to oppose and if possible thwart the policies of the Stuarts.

Gloucestershire emerged successfully from the Tudor period, its growing
population at most times adequately supplied by improved agriculture and
expanding trade: its towns larger and more efficiently administered; and
conditions of living for most people more secure and generally better than
they had been a hundred years before. The trading classes in the towns and
the gentry in the countryside effectively bridged the gap between the very
rich and the very poor, and cemented society in such a way that there were
no clear cut and divisive distinctions that could also be identified with and

thus aggravated by opposing economic and political interests. For the majority there was also a shared religion that even if not as powerful as the universal Catholic church had been during the Middle Ages was nevertheless a force making for unity.

The prosperity, resources and accessibility of the county were to make it of great strategic importance to both sides during the Civil Wars of the 17th century. The independence of its people and the variety of their interests determined that those who took sides during the war did so for purely personal reasons, neither on a class basis nor at the dictates of any faction. We said in the introduction that historical periods dovetail with each other and the interlocking of the 16th and 17th centuries is clearly illustrated in Gloucestershire history at that time. The continuation of manorial customs and abiding trust in the village church and its priest reflected the conservatism typical of rural communities, while the forward thrust of the ambitious newcomers in social life, and enterprising business men in the economic sphere represented an urge to move into the future. Mediaeval standards and practices inevitably became out of date in the changing and expanding world of the 16th century, yet the social and economic stability they had afforded for so long was indispensable as a starting point for progress into more modern times.

Bibliography

Manuscript Sources

In the Gloucestershire Record Office: Borough records indexed under Place Names: Parish records listed alphabetically in P index
In the Gloucester City Library: Hockaday Abstracts from the Records of the Diocese
At the Shakespeare Birthplace Trust, Stratford upon Avon: Stoneleigh MSS Gloucestershire Papers: Manorial Records

Contemporary Sources

W. Harrison, *The Description of England* (1577)
J. Leland, *The Itinerary of John Leland* (1535–1543)
J. Smith, *Men and Armour in Gloucestershire* (1608)
T. Wilson, *The State of England AD 1600*

Secondary Sources

R. Atkyns, *The Ancient and Present State of Gloucestershire* (1712)
S. Bindoff, *Tudor England* (1960)
J. Buxton, *Elizabethan Taste* (1983)
E.M. Carus-Wilson, *Mediaeval Merchant Venturers* (1954)
A.G. Dickens, *The English Reformation* (1964)
K. Esdaile, *English Church Monuments* (1946)
J. Finberg, *The Cotswolds* (1977)
B. Frith, *Gloucester Portraits*
J. Johnson, *Gloucestershire Towns* (1983)
D. Knowles, *The Religious Orders in England* (1959)
J.E. Neale, *Elizabeth I and her Parliaments* (1957)
P. Ramsey, *Tudor Economic Problems* (1963)
S. Rudder, *The New History of Gloucestershire* (1779)
Tanner, *Tudor Constitutional Documents* (1940)
Tawney and Power, *Tudor Economic Documents* (1924)
Victoria County History of Gloucestershire
W.B. Wilcox, *Gloucestershire 1590–1640* (1940)
P. Williams, *The Tudor Régime* (1979)
J. Youings, *Sixteenth Century England* (1984)

Acknowledgements

This book is largely based on manuscript sources, so my thanks go first to Record Offices and Libraries for producing the material I requested; in particular, I am grateful to Mr D. Smith and staff at the Gloucestershire Record Office; Dr R. Bearman and staff at the Shakespeare Birthplace Trust; and staff at the Bodleian and Gloucester City Libraries. The Librarians at Stow on the Wold, Moreton in Marsh and Cirencester have kindly made reference books available to me.

Other people have readily answered questions and supplied information and advice, including Dr Margaret Toynbee, Mrs Rosemary Verey, Mrs Mavis Batey, the late Mr David Verey, the Rev J. Lewis of Cirencester, and the owners of some of the houses mentioned in the text.

Many gave interested help while I was searching for illustrations, and I am particularly grateful to Mrs Barnard of Gloucester City Museum, Mr Francis Greenacre of Bristol Museum and Art Gallery, and Mr David Lowsley Williams. My special thanks go also to Mr W.A. Walker and Mr Bob Sharp who took photographs expressly for this book.

For gracious permission to reproduce photographs, I am indebted to: the Ashmolean Museum, the Bristol Museum and Art Gallery, Mr R.J. Baxter, Cambridge University Library, Country Life Magazine, Gloucester City Museum and Art Gallery, Gloucestershire Record Office, the Guildhall Library, Mr A.F. Kersting, Mr D. Lowsley Williams, the National Portrait Gallery, Oxfordshire County Libraries, the Paul Mellon Centre, the Shakespeare Birthplace Trust and the Trustees of the Bedford Estates and of Northleach.

Finally I should like to thank Miss Sybil Harris who typed the script, and the staff of Alan Sutton Publishing Ltd who have been unfailingly helpful throughout.

Index

Page references to illustrations are in italics.